HEALING BURNOUT

BURNOUT

WITH

ASTROLOGY

& TAROT

HEALING BURNOUT

WITH

ASTROLOGY & TAROT

A JOURNEY THROUGH THE DECANS OF THE ZODIAC

JACKIE HOPE

HAY HOUSE

Carlsbad, California • New York City
London • Sydney • New Delhi

Published in the United Kingdom by:
Hay House UK Ltd, The Sixth Floor, Watson House,
54 Baker Street, London W1U 7BU
Tel: +44 (0)20 3927 7290; Fax: +44 (0)20 3927 7291; www.hayhouse.co.uk

Published in the United States of America by:
Hay House Inc., PO Box 5100, Carlsbad, CA 92018-5100
Tel: (1) 760 431 7695 or (800) 654 5126
Fax: (1) 760 431 6948 or (800) 650 5115; www.hayhouse.com

Published in Australia by:
Hay House Australia Ltd, 18/36 Ralph St, Alexandria NSW 2015
Tel: (61) 2 9669 4299; Fax: (61) 2 9669 4144; www.hayhouse.com.au

Published in India by:
Hay House Publishers India, Muskaan Complex, Plot No.3, B-2,
Vasant Kunj, New Delhi 110 070
Tel: (91) 11 4176 1620; Fax: (91) 11 4176 1630; www.hayhouse.co.in

Text © Jackie Hope, 2024

Cover design: Claudine Mansour
Interior design: Karim J. Garcia

The moral rights of the author have been asserted.

A catalogue record for this book is available from the British Library.

Tradepaper ISBN: 978-1-78817-925-6
E-book ISBN: 978-1-4019-7274-5
Audiobook ISBN: 978-1-4019-7275-2

This product uses papers sourced from responsibly managed forests. For more information, see www.hayhouse.co.uk.

Printed and bound by CPI (UK) Ltd, Croydon CR0 4YY

TABLE OF CONTENTS

To the One who lights my soul on fire, this one's for You—an amazing person, full of potential, and ready to remember why you are here and who you are.

INTRODUCTION

A SONG AROUND THE SUN

Each of us carries trauma to varying extents, and this book uses the symbols of tarot and astrology to invoke the sun's healing powers, with the goal of restoring balance by becoming more acutely aware of the active and receptive energies flowing in our nervous system.

Like a plant gravitating toward light, our bodies strive for a homeostatic center. But just like a plant can grow off balance if light only enters through a side window, our emotional, mental, or spiritual center can skew if we are constantly exposed to traumatic environments, setting biological feedback loops to uphold this skewed state, causing what should be abnormal to become the new normal.

Medication can be employed to modify the set point in these feedback loops. Internal changes are also possible. Much like a personal trainer targets a muscle group on the left side to reestablish the right side's balance, symbolic tools like tarot and astrology can aid in realigning our mental patterns back to a desired set point. By recognizing emotional and thinking responses to different symbols, we begin to recognize our individual patterns that shape our behaviors. If there is a pattern we do not want, we can interrupt the pattern and reinstall a new one.

BURNOUT AS THE PRELUDE

Burnout occurs when our set point has deviated so much in a way that our body starts shutting down. Just like warning lights on a car, our body shows warning signs—first through changes in mood, behavior, and thoughts, then through minor acute illness, a pain here, a cold there, headaches, and weight gain—to chronic conditions such as persistent high blood pressure, heart disease, or cancer.

There have been many studies, articles, and papers naming the causes of burnout. Causes such as workload, lack of control (real or perceived), unmet expectations, isolation or too much community, injustice, and incongruent values are just a few.

Ultimately, in short, burnout indicates that there is something in your body or environment that is not in *agreement* with the safety, security, peace, joy, and love requirements of your nervous system. Thus, you are "threatened," and your nervous system responds accordingly, sends messages to your body and mind, as an indicator that you are operating out of your body's window of tolerance and are therefore "dysregulated."

These dysregulations take two general forms—too much "gas" on the nervous system or too much "brake."

The sympathetic nervous system, the accelerator of the body, puts the body into fight or flight—the body prepares to move, and to move quickly—manifesting in anxiety, aggression, impulsiveness, emotional outbursts, and chaotic responses.

Alternatively, the parasympathetic nervous system, acting as the brake of the body, puts the body into fawn or freeze states—ready to people-please or leave the situation—resulting in depression, daydreaming, or being overwhelmed or confused.

To heal and transform burnout into fuel and ultimately a fire that will propel you to move along the path you desire, we must move the mind, body, and spirit back into a place of safety. This is what some researchers call the "window of tolerance," or the

equilibrate or steady state of your nervous system. Spiritual practices may call this finding your "balance," finding your "heart
center," or finding "alignment." In the Christian tradition, the
religion of my ancestors, this can be described as "finding peace
by walking with Jesus." Ultimately, whatever words or symbols are
used to describe it, healing burnout is a returning home to Self.
It is a return to our bodies' innate ability to repair and restore in
the background of our lives, so that we may redirect our energy
toward generating abundance for ourselves and our communities.

THIS BOOK AS A HEALING MUSIC
FOR THE MIND-BODY-SOUL

While this book will cover many exercises, strategies, reflections, and mindset shifts to support you in healing and transforming burnout, ultimately, as a former burnt-out public high
school teacher, I found these two considerations to be a helpful
"compass" to help me return to a more steady state in my nervous system:

1. What would you do if every day were summer
   vacation? Ideally, you would respond with *exactly
   what I'm doing right now.*

2. How can you do more of what lights your soul
   on fire? Engaging with this question activates
   the intuition to lead you to where you need or
   want to go.

Healing and transforming burnout through the use of symbols and reflection is rooted in the progression found in frameworks such as Abraham Maslow's hierarchy of needs or Robert
Dilts's neurological levels. Ultimately, while these two frameworks
are debated and differ in tone and effect, these hierarchical frameworks suggest that there is a linear progress of needs—with certain needs being more foundational than others. First come basic
needs such as air, water, food, shelter, sleep, and clothing; then
accessing creative energy to needs such as safety, love, and esteem;
and then self-actualization or walking in purpose with purpose.

The decans framework is like these previous frameworks, as it recognizes the need for certain needs to build on one another. It is difficult to self-actualize if our time, money, energy, and resources are being exhausted to meet our basic needs of food, water, shelter, and clothing. However, the decans framework differs, as it suggests that we are always becoming something, that a walk with the Sun or a walk with the Divine or Self is always here—we just have to shift our mindsets and behaviors to get in agreement with it (as well as be open to practices such as gratitude for what we have in the present moment) while channeling the creativity to think differently about how we are using our time, money, resources, relationships, and energy stores.

INVOKING THE SACRED HEALING POWER OF THE SUN

Solar worship is a practice deeply rooted in human understanding of the natural world, and Jesus of Nazareth has been interpreted as a figure of solar worship by some scholars. One of the key characteristics of solar deities is their association with light, rebirth, and redemption, all of which are also commonly associated with Jesus in Christian iconography and ritual practices. Furthermore, the symbolism of the Sun itself can be found throughout Christian art and literature, from the halo around Christ's head to the imagery of the resurrection as a new dawn.

The cultural significance of Jesus as a figure of solar worship extends beyond Christianity, with many cultures and religions mirroring elements of the Jesus story into their own solar myths. Another solar deity is the Egyptian god Ra. Ra was revered as the embodiment of the Sun. The Egyptians believed that Ra created the world and brought about each new day, and they paid homage to him through elaborate rituals and ceremonies. They also believed that the pharaohs were descendants of Ra, giving them divine status.

In ancient Babylon, the Sun was revered as the god Shamash. Shamash was seen as the bringer of justice and truth, and worshippers would offer prayers and sacrifices to him in exchange for his blessings. The Babylonians also believed that Shamash was responsible for guiding the souls of the dead to the underworld.

Babylonian rituals surrounding solar worship involved offering incense and lighting fires to symbolize the Sun's warmth and energy. They also built temples in honor of Shamash, with the most famous being the Temple of Shamash in Sippar.

The Incas of South America worshipped the Sun as Inti, one of their most important gods. Inti was seen as the source of all life and energy, and the Incas believed that their emperor was a direct descendant of the Sun god. The Incas celebrated the winter solstice with the Inti-raymi festival, which involved sacrificing llamas and offering food and drink to Inti. They also built temples and other structures that were aligned with the Sun's movements, symbolizing their reverence for the Sun.

In Japan, the Shinto religion venerates the Sun goddess Amaterasu, who is believed to be the ancestor of the Japanese imperial family. Amaterasu is associated with fertility, prosperity, and power, and she is worshipped through various rituals and customs. One of the most significant events in Japanese solar worship is the Daijōsai ceremony, which takes place after a new emperor ascends to the throne. The ceremony involves offerings of food and drink to Amaterasu, symbolizing the emperor's connection to the Sun goddess. The Japanese also celebrate the summer solstice with the Yoiyama Festival, which includes bonfires and fireworks to mark the longest day of the year.

In yogic teachings of Shiva-Shakti—the Sun can be seen in the practice of kundalini yoga, the creative force arising from the root chakra. The awakening of this energy plays a central role and marks a transformation from asleep to awake, from blind to seeing, from child to adult. When we awaken the solar power of the kundalini, we become more acquainted with our spiritual powers or reason for being. Kundalini is described as the creative power for many of humanity's most enlightened teachers and leaders. Albert Einstein, for example, expressed that God-experience had supported him on his personal path. Even in Christianity, this coiled serpent at the bottom of the spine is referenced when in Corinthians, Paul talks about the union between two humans: "For it is better to marry than to burn with desire."

Over time, our understanding of Jesus as a solar deity has evolved alongside changes in religious and cultural beliefs. While some may view this interpretation as purely symbolic, others may see it to reconcile their faith with a broader understanding of the world and its natural rhythms. As we continue to explore the meaning of this interpretation, it remains an important part of the ongoing conversation around religion and spirituality.

THE SUN IN ASTROLOGY

In *The Archetypal Universe* by Renn Butler, the Sun is described as our conscious ego with impulses to express itself creatively—be it having children, creating music, starting a business, writing a book, playing chess, creating a workout routine, or coming up with a new take on an old idea.

The Sun symbolizes dynamism and potency. It's a self-sustaining powerhouse, fueling our world with light and warmth. On the other hand, the moon embodies receptivity. Unlike the sun, it doesn't produce its own light, but mirrors the sun's radiance, enabling us to marvel at the stars and their formations.

Often, we overlook the significance of the sun due to its unwavering presence; it's always there. Yet, when we disregard the sun's sacredness, we tend to stay indoors more, rely on artificial lighting, pull all-nighters, and live in discord with the sun's power.

THE DECANS AS A FRAMEWORK FOR SOLAR WORSHIP

The decans—also known as *faces*—are an ancient Egyptian method of dividing the zodiac's 10-degree sections, creating three 10-day intervals within each month. Each decan corresponds to a sign and a planet, containing its own manifesting power. There are 36 faces to the zodiac, and the decans describe their nature and power.

Ancient Egyptians had an idealized 360-day calendar. It consisted of 12 months, 30 days each, with 5 additional days added to the end of every year. Every 30-day month was divided into thirds, and each of these 10-day periods was associated with a fixed star. These groupings came to be known as the *decans* (from the Greek word *deka*, meaning 10).

Egyptian astrology was focused on the rising and culmination of the stars associated with the decans, which was called *diurnal rotation*. The decans were a precursor to the Hellenistic doctrine of 12 "places" (topoi)/houses. It is believed that the decans were originally used to keep time, alerting priests to begin performing religious ceremonies whenever the fixed star associated with that decan rose over the horizon. By the 4th century, the decans had also been assigned specific astrological significance. The earliest evidence of decans was found on coffin lids dating back to 2100 B.C.E.

Theresa Ainsworth, a classics scholar, described the decans as "a set of thirty-six stars or constellations selected by the Egyptians in the First Intermediate Period as a means of marking the progression of the hours during the night . . . Once Egypt became colonized by Hellenistic rulers, the decans were adapted into the imported Babylonian zodiac. Once incorporated into the Hellenistic astrological system, which synthesized elements of both Egypt and Mesopotamia, the decans were believed to influence human health through the bonds of cosmic sympathy—the idea that all celestial bodies impacted human life in one way or another."

In medieval astrology, Guido Bonatti likened the decans to "a [person] who is among unknown peoples such as happens with foreigners and the like, but [they] live among them by art and skill, or by service, or by any other craftsmanlike or lay art." Another commenter likened the decans as fine ornaments and clothing.

The Rider-Waite-Smith deck was illustrated by artist and mystic Pamela Coleman Smith, commissioned by A. E. Waite, and published by William Rider & Son in 1909. Over 100 years later, the deck has sold more than 100 million copies in 20-plus countries. It has stood the test of time and become one of the most influential and respected tarot decks. It is said that Pamela Coleman Smith illustrated the deck with the decanic associations in mind.

HOW TO USE THIS BOOK

This book can be used in many ways. The first way is to *move through the book at a pace and order that feels right to you*. Take a look at the table of contents and see what speaks to you.

Some other suggestions include:

- A yearlong devotional aligned to the zodiacal calendar

- 36 stand-alone devotionals over 36 weeks

- 108 daily devotionals (2–4 per week)

- Devotional at random

- To accompany the use of tarot or oracle cards or astrology as an idea-generation tool

- To accompany an in-depth study of the minor arcana

The reflections in this book are numbered. You can use them as reflections. You can pull one tarot card for each question to guide your thought processes. You can even use the planets if you are familiar with or have a background in astrology. Pull the transits for the moment you are asking the question and allow the planets to guide your intuition to the best answer.

THIS SONG IS FOR YOU

Burnout, especially when it manifests as physical illness, may make us feel like we have failed, but we have not. Even though it can feel like we will never recover, we will. Even when it feels like the Sun will never rise again, it will. Even though it's uncomfortable, periods of burnout provide the darkness—the womb—the fertile soil for us to separate from overload and sensory stimulation so we can pause, reset, and decide when, how, and where to reignite our fire. It is the intent of this book to be that secret space—the dark place—where you can repair your relationship with your passion, your energy, the Sun, and realign and reignite to get in agreement with who you want to be and what you want to create in this world.

THE DECANS OF ARIES

Exhausted
Broken
Unmotivated
Lost
Nowhere to go
A New World
But an Old Soul
Light a fire?
Attempted
Failed
No fuel
But the Divine
Lends
Light
Unbecoming
Illuminated
An end
Is a beginning
To
A New Life
Right there
Beyond
What is Known

ARIES I: BURNOUT as an INVITATION to HEALING

Two of Wands as Mars in Aries

We all have our own paths to walk. There are mountains and valleys. People come and people go. Some paths go left, some paths go right, some take us up, some take us down. What's right for you could be wrong for another. What's wrong for another could be right to you. Choose to define your life. Choose to let others define your life for you. That's okay, too. But make the effort to consciously choose for you.

BURNOUT ENCOURAGES YOU TO THINK DIFFERENTLY

"I just can't take this anymore and I'm tired."

There have been countless moments in my life when I've felt the weight of the phrase "I just can't take this anymore." Maybe you've had similar experiences. It could be after watching a distressing news story, enduring a job that drains your spirit, or being in a relationship with someone who hinders your growth and success. We've all been there. These are the moments of exhaustion and extreme stress, when our mental, physical, and spiritual capacities reach their limits, signaling that enough is *enough*.

In these instances, we have at least one thing to be grateful for—a nervous system alerting us to the conflict between the calling of our soul and our surrounding environment. The challenge, however, lies in our inability to envision a new, sustainable path once we recognize our current one as unsustainable. In such moments, we could heed Robert Frost's advice and choose "the road less travelled." Alternatively, we might follow the crowd, seeking comfort in numbers and social acceptance.

We are always engaging with the push-pull dynamics of individualism vs. collectivism, meaning, considering whether it is time to be selfish or selfless. Burnout occurs when we have become so set in a certain pattern that we have no option but change. Periods of burnout don't necessarily signify personal failure or indicate a need to work harder or be a "better" person. Rather, they sometimes signal a transition into a new phase of life. Each period of burnout is unique, varying in intensity and impact. What remains constant, however, is our desire to move beyond this state of exhaustion. It's as though the Universe is directly calling us, urging us to consciously connect with our bodies and become more aware of what we are creating.

Although our bodies are in a constant state of healing, burnout provides us with an opportunity to heal in ways that are tailored to our unique aspirations, needs, and circumstances. While we are all human, our genetic makeup, environment, and life experiences vary greatly.

This healing process can be challenging because it asks us not to emulate others but to forge our own path. Like an artist, we must gather fragments of experiences from various sources and assemble them in a way that doesn't follow a preset template but is guided by suggestions alone.

This process results in a world that is distinctly yours, designed to cater to your needs and those of its other inhabitants. The Universe is in a constant state of expansion, and so is our world. Despite periods of pruning, we continue evolving, building on the lessons of the past and leveraging advances in science and psychology to make better choices today. As we courageously engage in introspection and self-improvement, we become active contributors to a world where healing ourselves to heal the world is not just aspirational but entirely achievable.

Exercise: Reviewing Your Natal Chart

This book guides you on a transformative journey, using symbolism and archetypes as healing tools to overcome burnout. Among the myriad of symbols available, such as flowers, crystals, and runes, this book encourages you to delve into the universal symbols that exist in the stars and tarot, which will invite your inner knowing to rise up to the surface.

To embark on this journey, I invite you to use your map—a copy of your natal chart. This requires your birth date, time, and location. You can make use of a professional program like Astro-Gold, or opt for a free alternative like Astro-Charts.com.

If you're uncertain of your birth time or unable to find it, don't worry. You can seek guidance from a professional astrologer or alternatively, trust your intuition to choose a time or rising sign that resonates with you. Remember, this is about your personal journey toward healing and transformation, and your intuition is a powerful guide.

Card Reflection: Choosing Your Companions

In addition to your natal chart, tarot or oracle card decks can be useful companions. In periods of burnout, you likely have so many racing thoughts, that the cards help sort through these thoughts and through symbols and pictures, turn up the volume on your emotions so you can sort and process as you wish.

To select your card companions, ask yourself the following questions, jotting down your answers as you go. Do not try to solve any issues. Just reflect, observe, and vision your new life:

- What do I want to stay the same?

- What do I want to do differently?

- Where am I unsure of what I want?

- What has the Universe done for me lately? (Focus on the small things—they are always there.)

- Now looking at your answers above, find a tarot or oracle deck that speaks to you as a symbol of your healing journey through the decans. You can go in person or order online. See the appendix for a list of tarot and oracle decks that I used on my own healing journey. If you don't know where to begin, an oracle deck or the Rider-Waite Smith tarot is recommended.

Affirmation

I release the need for perfect and embrace the beauty of my present imperfection. I embrace a growth mindset and choose to see times of burnout as an opportunity to rest, repair, learn, and evolve.

HEALING WITH THE FOOL: CHOOSING TO DO DIFFERENT

One of the most powerful insights I've gained throughout my life is this: "There is no definitive right or wrong, merely choices and their subsequent effects or consequences." As a legal professional, I have witnessed the profound truth of this wisdom within the judicial system. Two cases, identical in almost every aspect, can diverge dramatically in their outcomes due to a single differing detail. The law remains constant, but its interpretation and application depend on the facts of the case.

The interpretation of law is influenced by the values held by the presiding judge or, in more complex cases, a panel of judges. This collective value system we call our "judiciary" ultimately shapes the enforcement, modification, or interpretation of laws over time.

Our personal value systems are formed through the choices we make and those made by the people around us. When we align our individual values with societal values, we make decisions that we perceive to be the "best" for any given situation at that moment.

When feelings of burnout start to overwhelm us, focusing our thoughts and actions on the concept of choice can help reinvigorate our minds, especially when emotional reactions or ingrained habits begin to dominate. Engaging with the idea of *choice* brings us back to the present moment. By living in the now, we acknowledge the past as unchangeable and recognize the future as a product of the intentional choices we make in the present. These choices shape who we are, who we aspire to be, the company we keep, the beliefs we hold, and the emotions we allow ourselves to experience.

There will be times when we feel powerless, frustrated by circumstances beyond our control. Sometimes, this perception is accurate. However, even in these moments, we have the power to choose how we respond. During periods of burnout, we can choose to focus on the aspects of our lives we can change. We can choose to learn something new or embark on a novel experience. Remember, the power of choice is always there, *somewhere*.

Exercise: Healing with the Fool: Notice, Name, and Neutralize

In tarot, the Fool card symbolizes a pivot point: endings, new beginnings, freedom, healing, decision-making, and the mystery of what lies ahead. The Fool's seemingly impulsive approach to adventure might appear reckless, but the Fool is ready to face the highs and lows that life's journey may bring. The Fool card is often linked with the planet Uranus, which represents disruption, exhilaration, and liberation through exploration. Governed by the element of Air, the element required to light a fire, the Fool possesses the mental agility needed to make swift decisions in the now. By applying the "observe, identify, neutralize" method with the Fool, you'll learn to focus on the present moment and understand how your choices can help you navigate through and heal from burnout as you journey back to your true self.

- **Observe:** Choose a peaceful and cozy spot where you can unwind without interruptions. Close your eyes and breathe deeply, grounding yourself in the present. Bring your awareness to your physical being. Observe the sensations within your body. Where do you sense warmth? Cold? Tension? Relaxation? What thoughts are occupying your mind?

- **Identify:** What emotions are surfacing? Can you link these feelings to a specific part of your body? As thoughts or emotions emerge, be aware of their existence. For instance, if you experience uncertainty or fear, acknowledge it. Silently label the emotion, saying something like, "I'm experiencing fear." Then, with a deep breath, envision dispelling that emotion, diminishing its control over you. If any thoughts or emotions become overwhelming, gently redirect your focus to the present moment.

- **Neutralize:** Ponder the concept of choice in the present moment. Like the Fool standing at the precipice, poised to leap into the unknown, think about the choices available to you right now. Which actions could bring you nearer to your goals and dreams? How do your decisions affect your future self? Let these reflections unfold.

Take a final deep breath, feeling a sense of healing washing over you. As you exhale, release any tension or stress you may be holding on to. Remember that, like the Fool, you have the freedom to embrace new beginnings and navigate the unknown with curiosity, creativity, and courage.

Card Reflection: Choosing Your Companion

Was there a particular thought or feeling that was hard to label and move on from? Could you sense the space in you that noticed and named what was happening? Consider choosing a companion card to illuminate a message that the Fool has for you.

Shuffle your deck and lay out three cards side by side. If you choose a companion card, place it between cards one and two.

1. How can this companion card help you along your healing journey?

2. What additional support or next step may be required?

3. Choose a third card if you need any additional messages or clarification.

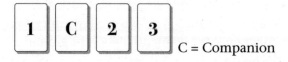
C = Companion

Affirmation

Whatever works best for me, works best.

BURNOUT AS AN INVITATION TO SYMBOL MEDICINE

One way to comprehend burnout is the body's incapacity to keep processing our lived experiences due to an overload of unprocessed emotions. Think of it as having too many unfinished tasks or, in modern terms, "too many tabs open." In their book, *Burnout: The Secret to Unlocking the Stress Cycle*, sisters and authors Emily and Amelia Nagoski propose that "emotions are like tunnels. If you journey through them, you find light at the end. Fatigue sets in when we become trapped in an emotion."

Engaging with symbols, archetypes, and images offers a unique way to delve into and process profound emotions that may be suppressed or stuck within us. They communicate directly with our subconscious mind, bypassing the conscious filters that limit our understanding of emotions. Renowned psychiatrist Carl Jung viewed symbols as a bridge connecting the conscious and unconscious realms, providing deep insights into our inner world. Conversely, Sigmund Freud highlighted symbolism's role in expressing suppressed desires and fears.

Symbols serve as universal conveyors of deeper psychological interpretations. For instance, the sun typically signifies life force, vigor, and enlightenment, while the moon embodies the unconscious mind, intuition, and feelings. Various emotions can be evoked by flowers; roses symbolize love and passion, while daisies denote innocence and purity. Animals also bear symbolic importance, with the lion signifying strength and bravery, and the butterfly embodying transformation and rebirth.

In therapeutic contexts, symbolism can be utilized to facilitate emotional exploration and processing. Dream analysis, for instance, interprets the symbols found in our dreams to provide insight into our unconscious yearnings, fears, and unresolved emotions. Art therapy provides a creative medium for expressing and exploring emotions via symbolic images. Guided visualization exercises use symbols to delve into the psyche's depths, revealing hidden emotions and beliefs. Many religions utilize symbolic narratives and symbols to explore our inner worlds.

Interacting with symbols gives us a renewed viewpoint on our emotions, allowing us to examine them in a non-aggressive and non-intimidating way. Symbolism offers a secure and transformative environment for self-reflection, healing, and personal development. It helps us connect with our subconscious mind, uncover unconscious patterns, and relieve emotional blockages, leading to heightened self-awareness and well-being.

However, it's critical to acknowledge the limitations of symbolism. Symbols are subjective and can have different interpretations for different people. Furthermore, relying exclusively on symbolism may not fully address the intricacies of complex emotions or traumatic experiences. Hence, it's beneficial to combine symbolism with other therapeutic strategies and seek professional advice when necessary.

Affirmation

I am open to receiving the wisdom and insights that symbols offer, trusting in their ability to support my healing process. I connect with nature as a symbol of renewal and rejuvenation, finding solace and inspiration in its gentle rhythms and beauty. I honor my emotions as valuable messengers, using symbols to explore and process them with compassion and understanding.

ARIES II: RESPONDING AS THE SOVEREIGN OF YOUR EXPERIENCE

Three of Wands as Sun in Aries

A new Earth is created by telling stories that inspire us to see both simplicity and nuance. Our stories may not apply to other people's lives, but our stories can connect us to others in a way judgment and separation cannot.

MIND WHERE YOU REACT

In times of stress and burnout, we often lose our ability to pause and appreciate the people and things around us. Our instinctive response to such threats is to either fight, flee, freeze, or appease. Rather than acting from a place of personal power—a space where our mind, heart, and soul work in harmony—we let our surroundings dictate our reactions.

Responses driven solely by emotion or instinct rob us of our power. These automatic reactions can be triggered by hidden wounds or unresolved issues. When we let our emotions control us instead of using them as feedback for our mind-body, we become victims of our surroundings. The key to liberation is aligning our emotional instincts with the structure of our minds and the wisdom of our souls. This alignment invites the Universe's magic into our lives, allowing us to co-create and manifest the life we were designed to live.

In addition, only relying on intuition or emotional responses can result in harmful biases. We *all* have biases formed by our personalities, past experiences, and associations. Factors like culture, religion, trauma, attachment styles, resources, societal systems, and the era we were born in shape these biases. Biases can lead us to places of perceived safety, security, and love, but they can also alienate or harm groups we perceive as "different." This exclusion breeds fear, intolerance, and violence, whether intentional or not.

While it's tempting to blame others for this harm, we gain more strength when we focus on improving, healing, or educating ourselves. If we're unconscious to our biases, we're working with incomplete information. By acknowledging our biases, we enhance our understanding of ourselves, which in turn strengthens our relationships with others.

On our path to healing and transformation, we must be willing to confront our biases and inspect how they influence our actions. We must question whether our current beliefs align with those we want to carry into the future (and why). Recognizing our biases allows us to challenge them dismantle them, and consciously create with them because are aware of our nervous system set point.

Exercise: Connecting with the Breath

Our bodies store stress. Because we are all different, how we handle and respond to stressful events is also different. When we use the power of our breath with intention, we can train the mind to get rid of unwanted stress. We can also sing or chant to release muscle tension in places where we need to put our thoughts in a more trancelike state. Working with our breath, whether it's through focus on the breath, mindfulness exercises, singing, or working with a doctor, can heal the link between our body and mind and bring us back into agreement with peace.

1. Come to a comfortable position.

2. Close your eyes to minimize distractions.

3. Breathe in and notice any places in your body or posture that are tense or not in the proper position. This could be shallow breathing, breathing through the chest, or resistance to breathing.

4. Adjust.

5. Breathe out.

6. Breathe in again.

7. Scan for remaining conscious tension.

8. Breathe out.

9. Continue until you feel like you want to be finished.

Consider how you can incorporate this practice as part of your wellness rituals. Work with professionals where you feel called.

Card Reflection: Neutralizing Biases by Greeting Your Cards

Biases are multifaceted. Like it or not, they shape our thoughts and actions. In his book *Why Don't They Get It? Overcoming Bias in Others (and Yourself)*, Brian McLaren outlines thirteen biases that our minds and souls knowingly interact with. McLaren emphasizes that biases aren't inherently good or bad. Rather, it's how we employ them that matters.

Biases often stem from favoring a single perspective over analyzing multiple viewpoints. Let's take confirmation bias as an example. This bias nudges us toward maintaining established beliefs. To combat this, regularly revisit your convictions. Engaging with astrology transits through a mentor who can provide diverse perspectives can be useful. Similar to how decomposing organic material enriches soil, the continuous breakdown and renewal of ideas can fertilize our creative minds. Successful businesses frequently use this strategy through systematic review processes.

Symbolic representations, like tarot cards or natal charts, can make it easier to address our biases by producing either a supporting, neutralizing, or opposing force to the tendencies of our mental scripts. Every card deck holds a "charge" that represents the author's set point. This charge is going to have an interaction with your mental energy field.

One of the ways I like "greeting" a new tarot or oracle deck is by reading the guidebook from the author, if available, and then categorizing each card into three groups based on my intuition: (1) Cards that bring me joy, (2) cards that irritate me, and (3) cards

I'm uncertain about. I then address my concerns with the cards that confuse or bother me until I can comfortably place them in the joy category. Joy here isn't about positivity or negativity. It's a neutral state where you can observe both the good and bad aspects of the card without judgment. If reviewing the entire deck seems daunting, no worries! You can start with the tarot cards representing the Aries decans—for example, the Emperor, the Tower, and the 2, 3, and 4 of Wands.

Finally, as an ethical matter, it's crucial to understand and disclose our biases before reading for others. This is why personally, I choose *not* to read for people. I can share my interpretations, but I do not place myself in a position to hold authority over another's life by claiming to be a channeler, or someone with supernatural gifts. I read the cards as the scripts run through my mind, for myself, but always retain a dose of healthy skepticism.

Affirmation

I choose to respond with curiosity even though my initial reaction may be judgment. I consciously open my heart to see safety where others may see danger. I ask thoughtful questions about myself and others instead of assuming. I have an opinion, but that opinion is subject to change.

CULTIVATING CURIOSITY WITH THE QUEEN OF WANDS

During periods of burnout, our minds tend to resort to judgment. When in survival mode, whether due to exhaustion or overwhelming stress, the mind must make swift decisions, often defaulting to categorization—leading to judgment—as a quick and easy solution.

However, curiosity demands a more substantial investment of energy. It isn't about choosing between familiar options or worrying about immediate financial concerns. Curiosity engages us in deeper contemplation, encouraging us to explore the philosophical aspects of life that exist beyond our immediate needs and desires.

In times of extreme fatigue and burnout, it becomes even more crucial to carve out time and space to transform judgment into curiosity. If we neglect this, we risk viewing the world through a monochrome lens, constrained by our biases, personal histories, and unchallenged assumptions.

The Queen of Wands tarot card serves as a powerful symbol of the transformative power of curiosity and the healing potential of moving beyond judgment. She beckons us to let go of preconceived ideas and approach each situation and interaction with an open heart and mind. By acknowledging the shared humanity in everyone we encounter, we can cultivate connection and understanding, which helps us transcend judgment and let compassion take root.

Exercise: Queen of Wands Tarot Meditation

Close your eyes and take a deep breath. Inhale slowly, filling your lungs with the air of possibility, and exhale, releasing any tension or judgment you may be holding on to. As you enter this guided meditation, allow yourself to open to the Queen of Wands energy.

Imagine a woman seated upon a magnificent throne, adorned with vibrant, fiery colors. She exudes confidence and radiance, her fiery hair flowing freely, and her eyes sparkling with intense curiosity. The Queen of Wands is a symbol of passion, creativity, and leadership. Her energy is magnetic and captivating, drawing others toward her with a warmth that embraces all who come into her presence.

Now, imagine yourself embodying the energy of the Queen of Wands. Feel the warmth of her presence envelop you as you step into her shoes. Visualize yourself standing tall, confident, and filled with a genuine curiosity about the world around you.

You find yourself walking along a beautiful path, surrounded by nature's abundance. The air is filled with the scent of blooming flowers and the gentle whispers of the wind. As you walk, notice how your senses awaken. Take a moment to observe the vibrant colors, the intricate details, and the subtle sounds that surround you.

As you continue along the path, you come across a gathering of diverse individuals. Each person carries their own story, their own joys and struggles. Instead of casting judgment, you open your heart and embrace curiosity. Approach each person with a compassionate gaze, eager to learn from their unique experiences.

Engage in conversations, truly listening to their words, and seeing the world through their eyes. Allow your curiosity to guide you as you ask questions, seeking to understand rather than to judge. Embrace the richness of human diversity, recognizing that each person holds wisdom and beauty within them.

As the meditation ends, take a moment to reflect on the lessons of the Queen of Wands. Repeat these affirmations silently or aloud, allowing them to resonate within your being:

- I release judgment and embrace curiosity in all my interactions.
- I recognize the humanity in others, fostering connection and understanding.
- I approach every situation with an open mind and a compassionate heart
- I delight in the diversity of the world, celebrating the wisdom each person holds.
- I am confident in my ability to lead and inspire others through my genuine curiosity.

When you are ready, gently bring your awareness back to the present moment. Take a deep breath, feeling the energy of the Queen of Wands still resonating within you. Carry her lessons of embracing curiosity, acceptance, and compassion toward humanity into your everyday life, spreading warmth and healing wherever you go.

Card Reflection: Message from the Queen of Wands

Choose a tarot or oracle card at random. This card represents the message that the Queen of Wands has for you.

Affirmation

I choose to be curious about everyone's story, knowing that behind every action and word, there is a human being with their own perspective, fears, hopes, and struggles. I celebrate the diversity of humanity, appreciating the richness that different backgrounds, cultures, and experiences bring to my community.

ARIES III: HEALING ENERGY

Four of Wands as Venus in Aries

The collective energy is measured by the central tendency of its individual voices. Change the individual voice, and in turn, the vibration of the collective will be adjusted. We will grow into the people we want to become if we affirm the person we are becoming today.

HEALING BEGINS IN THE MIND

We are who we are, in part, because of the energy we invite into our lives, starting with the words we mentally consume and express.

The person we will be tomorrow begins with the words we speak today. Words hold vibrational power. They carry energy that can shape waves and matter, both seen and unseen. The world we want to manifest begins with the words we speak. If we want to create a world where we experience more creative power, joy, and love—rather than crisis, discord, and hate—one of the places to begin is by examining the words we invite into our experience.

The collective forces—laws, society, politicians—may be the soil, but words are the seeds we plant to become the medicine for our healing. Bringing something into existence begins with *speaking* it into existence. So many people look at individual and collective situations and say, "The politicians are at fault." While these systems may have their flaws, concentrating solely on their shortcomings and neglecting their successful aspects can lead to a disregard for our ancestors' contributions. This narrow perspective can also result in a lack of empathy for the challenging situations they had to navigate to shape the world we live in today.

The future we manifest depends on the words we use today. A just future is created by balancing venting about a problem with grounded action that contributes to solving that problem.

When confronted with societal issues that displease you, consider altering the way you articulate your observations. Rather than resorting to generalizations such as "politicians are terrible," dedicate an hour of your day to watch a live stream of your legislative body. This will give you insight into their roles and the multiple competing priorities they have to balance. Instead of declaring, "The healthcare system is broken," express it as, "The healthcare system is life-saving, but there are opportunities for improvement and nuance."

In both government and business, it's often the individuals in power, not necessarily the systems and tools, that shape outcomes. It's possible our ancestors inherited a system refined over thousands of years, and now it's simply time for evolution, not demolition. The first step lies in your mindset, the language you employ, and the actions you take.

Exercise: Rewriting a Mental Script

Write down one script that keeps playing over in your mind that you would like to change. How can you rewrite this script in a way where you can be the solution to the problem that you've identified? How may the placement of Mercury in your chart tone the way you communicate with yourself?

Card Reflection: Minding Your Words

Consider the words that you speak about issues or problems in your workplace, your local community, or society at-large. Shuffle your deck and lay out six cards according to the spread below.

1. What are my current words calling into existence?

2. What do I need to keep the same about the words I speak?

3. What words should I change?

4. Obstacles to this change?

5. What support do I need to have?

6. What are my next steps?

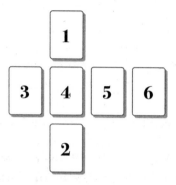

Affirmation

I was who I said I was. I am who I say I am. I will be who I say I will be.

A COMPASS FOR THE PERSON WHO WANT TO BECOME: THE 12 HOUSES

Astrological houses play a crucial role in astrology, each one illuminating distinct aspects of our existence, offering insights into our character, experiences, and untapped potential. There are 12 houses or places, each carrying its unique significance and interpretation.

The first house represents our identity and self-expression, while the second house focuses on our resources and values. The third house relates to communication and learning, and the fourth house signifies our home and family life. The fifth house is associated with creativity and romance, while the sixth house pertains to health and work. The seventh house revolves around partnerships and relationships, and the eighth house delves into transformation and shared resources. The ninth house explores higher education and spiritual pursuits, while the tenth house represents career and public image. The eleventh house symbolizes social connections and aspirations, and the twelfth house signifies spirituality and the subconscious.

Astrological houses can be effectively used in writing affirmations to manifest specific desires or enhance personal growth. By aligning affirmations with the corresponding astrological house, you can create a deeper connection with your intentions and increase the manifesting power of your affirmations.

For example, someone looking to enhance their career prospects may focus on affirmations related to the tenth house, such as "I am successful and fulfilled in my chosen profession" or "Abundance flows effortlessly into my professional life." Similarly, affirmations related to the fifth house, such as "I attract love and joy into my romantic relationships" or "I express my creative talents freely and confidently," can aid in cultivating fulfilling partnerships and creative endeavors.

A declaration, or affirmation, is a certain kind of energy that we can bring into our lives to make it more like what we want. The first person to use affirmations, which involves saying the same words every day, was the French psychologist Émile Coué. At the beginning and end of each day, he would ask his patients to say, "Every day, in every way, I'm getting better and better." It worked to say this. It changed the way his patients thought unconsciously and helped bring their mental energies into equilibrium.

When we declare our desires, we shift our mental energy in a way to break down barriers to creating our desired reality. And even when we feel our desires are not manifesting the way we would like them to, the Universe often gives us something even better—what we need for our soul's evolution.

Exercise: Writing Affirmations

Write a list of affirmations that describes who you are becoming. Repeat the affirmations daily, multiple times a day if you wish.

When writing the affirmations, consider the following tips:

- Write them in the affirmative (that is, "I am strong.") instead of the nonaffirmative ("I am not weak.").

- Write affirmations in the present tense, describing who you are becoming (that is, "I am strong." versus "I will be strong.").

- Use a card deck to inspire your affirmations. There are also ready-made affirmation decks that you can use.

- To personalize affirmations based on astrological houses, you can consult your birth chart to understand which houses are most influential in your life. Consider the ruling planet and sign of each house—they can provide further insights into creating effective affirmations. By incorporating the energy and themes associated with the relevant astrological house, affirmations become more personalized and resonant, leading to a greater manifestation of intentions.

Reflection: Yes, More, Please

Brainstorm qualities you would like to have more of in your life. If you wish, use a tarot or card deck to help.

1. When do you feel most vivid, energized, engaged?

2. What is the common thread that connects these patterns together?

3. What one action can you take to move closer to the person you are becoming?

Affirmation

I affirm who I am, what I want, and my ability to attract what I want, in service of the greatest and highest good for all.

MAP THE VISION FOR YOUR NEW LIFE WITH YOUR ASCENDANT

In astrology, the Ascendant, also known as the Rising Sign, symbolizes the zodiac sign that was rising on the eastern horizon at the precise moment you were born.

Generally speaking, the sign of the Ascendant reveals the individual's outward traits, physical appearance, and initial reactions to people and situations. It's the persona we project to the world. For instance, a person with a Leo Ascendant may display confidence, charisma, and a natural propensity for leadership. However, it is important to note that these qualities may be mitigated by other placements or transits in the natal chart.

For example, the Ascendant can be influenced by the angles that other planets make with the Ascendant. These angles are also known as "aspects." The aspects formed between the Ascendant and other planets shed light on how different energies interact, shaping an individual's overall character. For example, if the Ascendant forms a harmonious aspect with Venus, it may indicate a charming and diplomatic nature, enhancing one's social interactions.

Understanding the Ascendant is essential for gaining insight into the self. It provides a starting point for self-discovery, helping individuals become more aware of their strengths and weaknesses. By analyzing the Ascendant's sign, house, and aspects, you can establish a vision for your life and align your actions accordingly.

Embracing a vision is like a compass that can support navigation on your healing journey. A vision transcends simple goals or objectives; it encompasses the big picture and inspires direction. It propels you to act and bolsters resilience in the face of adversity. Esteemed authors like Stephen Covey (*The 7 Habits of Highly Effective People*) and Wayne Dyer (*The Power of Intention*) advocate that possessing a vision is pivotal to personal growth and achievement.

Just as a seed has an inner blueprint for the plant it is to become, a person needs a vision to shift their life into one of wholeness and abundance instead of lack and scarcity. Without a vision, you can easily fall prey to indecision and lack of focus, blame yourself for not doing the thing you want to do, and fall into a cycle of shame.

Exercise: Create a Vision with Your Ascendant Sign

Start by researching the characteristics associated with your Ascendant sign, or the sign that governs the first house of your natal chart. The Ascendant is calculated using your precise birth time, date, and location. Research information about the traits, strengths, weaknesses, and behaviors commonly attributed to your Ascendant. This will provide you with insights into your external personality and how you interact with the world. If you are familiar with your Ascendant already, consider learning more about your Ascendant from a new book or teacher.

You can use the Ascendant to understand the people that you attract in your life. You can also use the Ascendant to reflect on your needs and desires in relationships. For example—and know that this could be an oversimplification—if you have a Libra Ascendant, you may seek harmony, balance, and intellectual stimulation from your partnerships. Recognizing these patterns can aid in forming healthier and more fulfilling connections. The Ascendant also holds significance in one's emotions and psychology. It can reflect how an individual copes with their emotions and their approach to personal growth. For example, a person with a Scorpio Ascendant may have intense emotional reactions and a deep desire for cathartic experiences.

Card Reflection: Setting Intentions

Use your tarot or oracle cards to set an intention for the day, week, month, or season that is aligned to your vision. Consider using the tarot signifier card for your Ascendant sign to guide your reflection. Correspondences can be found in the appendix. You can also choose a signifier card consciously or at random. Shuffle your deck and lay out five cards according to the spread below.

1. What energy would you like to embody?
2. What do you want to keep doing in the present moment?
3. What do you want to stop doing in the present moment?
4. What additional support, tools, or resources do you need?
5. What next step can you take to move toward healing?

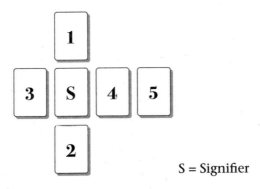

S = Signifier

Place the signifier card in your workspace or altar. When your intention has become reality, remove the card from this area.

Affirmation

The innate qualities of my Ascendant sign support me in navigating life's challenges with grace, ease, and unwavering strength.

THE DECANS OF TAURUS

Experience
Stored in the body
Revealing the codes
Of Relationship that we have
With ourselves
And with each other

Stars and scars
From our parents
Our environment
Our past lovers
Our experiences
The places we love
The objects we allow
In our personal Universe

Gratitude and affirming
Who we are
In the present moment
Releases us from our past regrets
And anxiety about the future

You are pure
You are holy
You just need to remember
Who you are
And connect it
With who you are becoming

Powered by the Sun
We begin to heal ourselves
And develop the capacity
To tell our stories
To contribute to
The cycle of healing, adapting, and evolving
Ourselves
Each other

And our communities

TAURUS I: YOU'RE COMING OUT

Five of Pentacles as Mercury in Taurus

Disempowerment occurs when we override our instincts, desires, and intuition with collective opinions that do not match the desire of our soul. Releasing expired labels opens space for us to take on something new and more congruent with our desires. While our personal desires will be regulated by the collective, aligning our actions with our core values is more likely to create a positive energy that can be exchanged with others.

PLANT THE SEEDS FOR THE PERSON YOU ARE BECOMING

Just as a seed absorbs water, puts down roots, and sprouts through the soil toward the light, so we are when we recognize our burnout, set a new direction for our lives, and shift the labels we carry to labels that give us energy, instead of draining our energy. Our labels give us insight into who we are right now so we can decide what to keep, what to discard, and what to consider, as we shift into a different vibration.

Seeds can be unpredictable in their early stages, and not every seed breaks the soil to become a sprout. Likewise, in our early stages of recovering, healing, and transmuting burnout, all we can do is place the seed in a nourishing environment and request the Universe to support its growth. The process of letting go, trying on, and putting on new labels can be simple—or difficult. We often feel as if we are an old soul in a new world. Just as many seeds do not make it the whole way to harvest, so many ideas and labels may not be the ones that fit us long term. And that's okay. Keep engaging with process, take a break when you need to, partner with people when you feel called, but always keep the end goal—to become the person you want to become—in mind.

As we reconsider our categorizations, let's take into account everything around us—the entities traditionally classified as living, such as plants and humans, and those typically deemed nonliving, like tarot cards, books, and household items. While we differentiate between nonliving and living things based on various characteristics, including the ability to grow and reproduce independently, it is important to acknowledge that both are ultimately composed of atoms. These atoms may be held together by varying degrees of force. Some configurations of atoms, found in living organisms, possess an inherent creative potential that allows them to interact with their environment. On the other hand, other groupings of atoms, seen in nonliving objects, have a creative potential that helps maintain balance among living entities. Similar to the checks and balances in our government system, nonliving and living things work together in a symbiotic relationship, inspiring creativity while also restraining any excessive tendencies of the other.

As a mystical practice, women have embodied this truth by counting seeds that evolved into beads. Where meditation has been a primarily masculine discipline tied to the rising and the setting of the Sun, circular Earth-based bead practices seem to have evolved from women as they collected seeds, nuts, and beans. These practices led to the evolution of rosaries and *mala* beads—beads that could be worn around different parts of the body that would support the wearer in engaging in a living meditation, rather than one prescribed at certain times of day.

Exercise: Adopt a Bead Practice

How can you incorporate a bead practice to align your mind to the reality you seek to create? Consider what form works best for you. The rosary is a traditional 59-bead form that has been followed for centuries by people across the world. The book *The Way of the Rose* by Clark Strand and Perdita Finn explores the ancient practice of the rosary, emphasizing its relevance and transformative power in contemporary spiritual practices. The prayers associated with these beads can be replaced with Buddhist sutras or other mantras. Consider shifting the words to better reflect what your intuition is guiding you to create in your physical reality.

Card Reflection: On Labels

Shuffle your deck and lay out five cards according to the spread below.

1. What labels do you currently wear?
2. What labels do you want to keep?
3. What labels do you want to discard?
4. What labels are you unsure about?
5. What next step can you take?

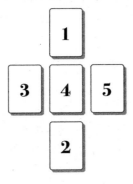

Affirmation

I recognize the value of all things, living and nonliving. I see all in devotion to the cycles of nature: the water cycle, the process of photosynthesis, the cycle of soil regeneration. Even though my seeds are planted in the dark, they know intuitively how to make their way back up to the light.

FIND THE PROPER SOIL FOR YOUR DREAMS

In the book of Genesis, there is a story of Joseph, a dreamer, who was adorned by his father with a coat of many colors, and who was born in a location to predict, adapt, and prepare for environmental challenges. In the story, Joseph's brothers threw him into a pit. Maybe his brothers were jealous because he was the favorite child, maybe his brothers were scared, or maybe his brothers thought he was crazy. In any event, Joseph, who was the solution to their agricultural problems in the region, was outcast and sent to a different land.

In this land, Joseph still had dreams, but instead of being ridiculed and mocked, he was accepted and gained favor with political leadership because of his insights. Because the person with the greatest power had the humility and curiosity to listen to a dream from a foreigner, their people were able to prepare for the upcoming famine and not only survive but thrive to the point they were able to store surpluses to sell to people who did not prepare for famine and natural disaster.

The ironic part of this story is that the people who failed to recognize Joseph's value to the collective were the people who knew him the best—his own family. Joseph was sold into a completely different culture and people to not just help them, but to use their resources and organization to help his family as well. Perhaps the Divine was guiding this journey all along, as reconciliation. We will never know for sure, but the moral of the story is this: be who you were created to be, unapologetically. Keep the dream and allow the Universe to take care of the rest.

Exercise: Exploring Dreams with the Hemp Plant (Cannabis sativa)

Dreams are a fascinating aspect of human experience, offering a glimpse into the mysterious realm of the subconscious mind. Psychologists believe that dreams serve a variety of purposes, including processing emotions, consolidating memories, and providing insights into our inner world. Interpreting symbols that appear in dreams can offer valuable insights into our psyche. For example, encountering water in a dream might represent emotions and the depths of the subconscious. Flying could symbolize a sense of liberation or the desire for freedom. By exploring these symbols and archetypes, we can gain a better understanding of our fears, desires, and unresolved issues.

Research has shown that hemp plants, specifically the cannabinoids found in them, can positively impact the quality of dreams. CBD, a non-psychoactive compound derived from hemp, has been studied for its potential to reduce stress and anxiety, providing a conducive environment for more peaceful and fulfilling sleep. By incorporating hemp into various practices, such as brewing herbal teas or utilizing its essential oils in aromatherapy, individuals can tap into the therapeutic benefits of the plant. The active chemicals in hemp interact with receptors in the brain, potentially leading to more vivid and meaningful dream experiences. Exploring dreams with the aid of hemp opens an opportunity for self-discovery and personal growth, allowing us to delve deeper into our subconscious minds. As we navigate the dream realm, we may gain insights, process emotions, and unlock hidden aspects of our psyche. By harnessing the properties of hemp, we can enhance our sleep quality, nurture our well-being, and embark on a journey of profound exploration within our own dreamscape. As with any medicinal herbs, consult a physician to make sure that you can integrate it healthfully in your life.

Reflection: Exploring Dreams

1. What is a dream you would like to explore?

2. What are the underlying emotions, thoughts, and beliefs coming to the surface in this dream?

3. What is a longing or unfulfilled aspiration or need that is being revealed by this dream?

4. What message does this dream have for you?

5. What support do you require?

6. Next step?

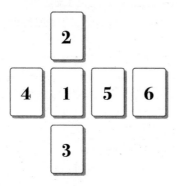

Affirmation

Just as a flower needs sunlight and water to blossom, my dream needs the nourishment of the right environment to flourish.

TAURUS II: YOUR BODY
IS YOUR TEMPLE

Six of Pentacles as Moon in Taurus

As I breathe in, I receive life from the collective while giving life to my individual body. As I breathe out, I give life to the Earth while receiving cleansing for my body. Getting in agreement with the Universe means syncing with its giving-and-receiving flow.

YOU ARE YOUR OWN SOURCE OF LOVE, JOY, AND HAPPINESS

We all seek to be loved and accepted by others. According to a study on the neuroendocrinology of love, love can be defined as an "emergent property of an ancient cocktail of neuropeptides and neurotransmitters." Often, love begins when an individual starts to see another as somehow special and unique. This leads to focused attention on the other, the minimizing of the other's faults, and separation anxiety when apart, along with dependence, empathy, sacrifice, obsessive thinking, and the desire to stay together at all costs. Rejection by the object of desire can trigger protest, rage, resignation, and despair.

This research relates to the idea of attachment styles. There are three attachment styles: anxious, avoidant, and secure. Anxious people tend to despair over the other. On the other hand, avoidant people try to minimize closeness because they equate intimacy with a loss of independence, perhaps because they have been hurt too many times before and see love more in themselves instead of in close relationship with others. Finally, secure people tend to know how to flow through seasons of intimacy and independence to improve their own individual sense of resilience—their own inner knowing or internal compass that is not reliant on the opinions, concerns, love, or care of others.

It is finding this sense of "security" that forms the basis for many of the world's religions. For example, in Christianity there is the idea of "accepting Jesus Christ as our savior." "Accepting Christ" is accepting the idea that we have accepted the wellspring of divinity to reside in our own heart; therefore, we choose to depend on others, but we are also at peace when it is time for us to be alone. In Buddhist philosophy, this idea is nonattachment and the middle way. This middle way invites us to engage with our experiences with flexibility and without fixation on achieving a specified thing in a specified way. A similar idea is found in the Bhagavad Gita 5.10: "One who performs his duty without attachment, surrendering the results unto the Supreme Lord, is unaffected by sinful action, as the lotus is untouched by muddy water."

Turning to spirituality or religion, however, is sometimes not the only answer and can cause more harm than good. In these cases, sometimes consulting a medical professional that you feel drawn to—be it allopathic medicine or nonallopathic medicine—will help you work with the energies flowing in your body in research-based, predictable, results-oriented ways, such as adjustments in diet, supplementation, or scientifically validated inquiry frameworks.

There are shadows to attachment just like there are shadows to extreme individuality. But when we choose to love ourselves, accept who we are in the present moment, choose to act, and be the ultimate source of peace, joy, and love in our lives, we can find an eternal wellspring of contentment within and at One with the Universe and Nature itself.

Exercise: Morning Pages and Artist Dates

Engaging in artistic practices can be another way that symbols show up as color, texture, and body movement. When you engage with your emotions, you can unlock creative potential. This idea forms the basis for Julia Cameron's book, *The Artist's Way*. There are two practices, in particular, that I found useful on my own healing journey.

- **Morning Pages.** At the heart of the book lies the concept of morning pages, a daily practice of writing three pages of stream-of-consciousness thoughts. This practice serves as a powerful tool to clear the mind, release self-doubt, and tap into the wellspring of creativity within. Cameron emphasizes that consistent engagement with morning pages cultivates self-awareness, nurturing the artist's inner voice and fostering a stronger connection to one's own creative instincts.

- **Artist Dates.** Cameron encourages readers to schedule regular solo excursions to explore new experiences, indulge in creative inspirations, and rekindle the joy of play. These artist dates serve as a wellspring of inspiration, providing fresh perspectives and invigorating the creative spirit.

What is one step you can take today to create a more ideal environment for more love, joy, and happiness in your life? Consider what *truly* lights your soul on fire and do that.

Card Reflection: Painting with Tarot

Begin by choosing an artistic activity that you feel drawn to. It could be painting, drawing, sculpting, writing, singing, dancing, or any other form of creative expression. Set an intention for this exercise—to create love and foster a deeper connection with yourself and others through your artistic expression using the tarot as your muse. After the card reflection, choose a time to start engaging in your chosen artistic activity. Allow yourself to freely express your emotions, thoughts, and desires through your creation. Shuffle your deck and lay out nine cards according to the spread below.

1. Signifier card for the activity.
2. How will engaging in this activity make you feel?

3. Color, symbol, or theme to incorporate?

4. How can you express self-love and acceptance during this activity?

5. How does this activity help you celebrate your uniqueness?

6. How can you create connections and cultivate love with your art?

7. What additional inspiration might you need?

8. Let this next card also provide additional inspiration.

9. What next steps should you take?

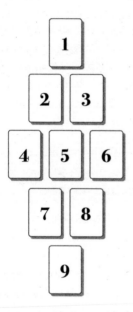

Affirmation

I embrace the joy of the creative process, letting go of self-judgment and allowing my inner artist to express freely.

SYMBOLIC ADORNMENT WITH THE
HIEROPHANT AND THE EMPRESS

Adornment is a universal language of self-expression, transcending cultural boundaries and societal norms. People have adorned themselves for various reasons, whether to display power and status, unleash their creativity, honor spiritual beliefs, or align their external reality with their internal reality. Body adornment, through tattoos, jewelry, body paint, and elaborate costumes, has served as a medium of communication, allowing individuals to convey their identity, express their emotions, and celebrate their personal style.

For example, in my Pacific-Islander lineage, tattooing was so sacred in Samoa that tattoo artists were of significant stature and held hereditary and privileged positions. Christian missionaries, unfamiliar with the practice of tattooing, because adornment in their culture was accomplished through jewelry, tried to suppress tattooing because they saw it as a work of darkness. However, for young Samoan men, tattooing was a rite of passage to manhood. In the Philippines, traditional Cordilleran tattoo practices are prevalent. Cordilleran is a term used for a person of the hill tribes of Luzon, an island in the Philippines. The Cordillera region of northern Philippines is the ancestral domain of the Igorot. Igorot tattooing was a very serious religious experience and was said to attract spirits that could protect or destroy a community.

However, there are some groups of people who see tattooing in the opposite light. For example, Jewish people rarely tattooed their bodies, as it was prohibited by Mosaic law. This belief extended to the Jews who followed the teachings of Jesus and were eventually called Christians. While there were religious tattoos found in Christianity, often they were souvenir tattoos of crosses on the arms of Crusaders during pilgrimages to the Holy Land.

Just as we all have unique body chemistries and emanate unique energy blueprints, so our choice of adornment will be different. For some people, the fixed nature of a permanent tattoo is necessary. For others, a temporary tattoo is what is needed. And still, for others, periodic interchanging of jewelry and not wearing jewelry allows them to flow with the more mutable nature. And still for others, adornment can come through the style and color of clothing they wear.

Exercise: Adorning Your Body with the Hierophant and the Empress

The themes of symbolic body adornment are also found in the Empress and the Hierophant. The Empress, with her embodiment of feminine power and connection to nature, mirrors the historical use of body adornment to honor goddesses, fertility rites, and the celebration of the life-giving forces within the world. The adornments worn by those who embraced the Empress's essence spoke of their reverence for the cycles of life, their connection to the earth, and their embrace of their own creative potential.

Alternatively, the Hierophant's symbolic body adornment reflects the rich tapestry of religious and spiritual traditions throughout history. Adornments such as sacred symbols, robes, and ceremonial jewelry have been used by spiritual leaders and practitioners to signify their role as intermediaries between the earthly realm and the divine. These adornments not only denoted spiritual authority but also served as visual reminders of the wisdom, rituals, and teachings passed down through generations.

The symbolic body adornment represented by the Tarot Empress and Tarot Hierophant cards highlights the profound relationship between personal expression, spirituality, and the embrace of our natural instincts. It reminds us that adornment is not merely superficial; it is a vessel through which we connect with ourselves, our environment, and the greater mysteries of life. Like those who adorned themselves throughout history, we too have the power to honor our creative energy, seek spiritual guidance, and manifest our inner truths through intentional adornment.

Consider your clothing and accessories. What brings you joy? What annoys? What adornments do you intentionally add to your body? Are they fixed or mutable? Consider placement, type of metal or ink used, and design. Gold often invokes the energy of action. Silver invokes receptive energy. Act where you feel called to act. Compare this to the placement of Venus in your birth chart.

Card Reflection: Adornment Inspiration

Take the Emperor and the Hierophant cards. Place them next to each other. Choose a third card that will give you insight on the connection between the two and the clothing, symbols, and accessories you choose to adorn your body with. Draw a fourth card if you would like guidance on any next steps. Continue drawing cards if you would like to request from your intuition some original designs for adornments or clothing.

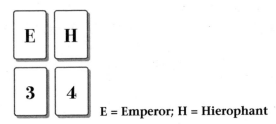

E = Emperor; H = Hierophant

Affirmation

I celebrate the beauty of my body and honor it by adorning it in ways that make me feel truly authentic and aligned with my true self.

TAURUS III: LEARNING FROM NATURE

Seven of Pentacles as Saturn in Taurus

No matter what, you are enough. You are enough when you feel like you're enough. You are enough when you don't feel like you're enough. You're enough when all you want to do is sleep through the day. You're enough when your heart has been hurt by someone you love. You are enough when you stand in front of the mirror and don't like yourself. You're enough when you're exhausted but didn't finish your to-do list. You're enough when you feel like you're not. Be kind to yourself.

THE THREE SISTERS

In Native American agriculture and culinary traditions, the three crops of corn, beans, and squash are known as the Three Sisters. By themselves they can stand, but not as strong. But when planted together, their individual imperfections become the fertilizer for each other's growth.

Corn grows tall for the beans so they can grow without being outcompeted by the squash vines. The beans provide nitrogen as fertilizer and stabilization for the corn during winds, but they also connect with the microscopic rod of *Rhizobium* bacteria, a completely different biological organism, to be a channel between two worlds. The large leaves of the squash plants shade the ground to retain soil moisture and prevent weeds.

Even after harvest, the Three Sisters maintain their collaboration—corn provides the carbohydrates, beans provide the protein, and squash provides vitamins that neither the corn nor beans possess.

The Three Sisters teach us that none of us have it all. We are created to work in co-creative partnership with people who are similar but also different from us. When we try to do everything ourselves, we may be able to grow, but we may miss the opportunity to flourish.

Exercise: Identifying Your Collaborators

Identify potential collaborators by making a list of individuals who possess complementary skill sets or expertise that align with your creative goals. Consider colleagues, friends, acquaintances, or professionals in your field who exhibit creativity and a willingness to collaborate. Also consider natal chart placements that come up a lot for you in chance encounters.

Affirmation

I believe in the power of collaboration with complementary skill sets, knowing that by working together, we can accomplish more than we ever could alone.

NATURE ISN'T NECESSARILY PERFECT

Nature, in its infinite wisdom, does not always conform to our predefined notions of "natural" or "organic." A closer look at the periodic table of elements reveals that the line between organic and inorganic compounds is not so much a judgment of perfection versus imperfection, but rather a matter of presence or absence of carbon atoms. By acknowledging this and moving beyond the binary of natural versus artificial, we can begin to appreciate the intricate complexity and value inherent in both types of compounds.

Historically, many organic compounds have been labeled as "natural" due to their widespread occurrence in life forms, while inorganic compounds were deemed "artificial." This dichotomy, however, oversimplifies the true essence of these compounds. The key difference lies in the carbon atoms forming the structural backbone of organic compounds, which are mostly absent in inorganic ones. This does not suggest one category is superior or perfect compared to the other; instead, it underscores their distinct properties, applications, and effects.

Organic compounds form the bedrock of biological systems and find usage across a spectrum of applications. They encompass vital molecules like carbohydrates, lipids, proteins, and nucleic acids—the fundamental building blocks of life. You'll also find organic compounds in everyday items such as plastics, fuels, and medicines, underscoring their versatility and complexity, and making them indispensable across various sectors.

Inorganic compounds, though devoid of carbon atoms, are far from imperfect or less valuable. They're integral to numerous processes and applications. Comprising minerals, metals, salts, and acids, inorganic compounds are vital across industries like electronics, construction, and energy production. Elements like iron, copper, and gold have been harnessed by humans for millennia, fueling technological progress and societal advancement.

Rather than categorizing compounds as perfect or imperfect based on their organic or inorganic nature, it's crucial to celebrate the diversity and symbiotic relationship of both types. Both organic and inorganic compounds can be beneficial or harmful, natural, or synthetic, depending on their specific characteristics and uses. It is through recognizing and leveraging the unique properties of each compound that we can heal and transform ourselves and our communities.

Exercise: Embracing the Entire Table of Elements

Begin by drawing a line down the center of your journal page. Label one side "Organic" and the other "Inorganic." On the Organic side, list aspects of your life that feel natural, fluid, and life-giving—these could be relationships, activities, or personal qualities that you associate with growth and vitality.

On the Inorganic side, list elements of your life that feel structured, solid, and stable. These could be routines, habits, or characteristics that ground and anchor you. Reflect on how these elements balance each other in your life. Contemplate how you can appreciate and harness the unique properties of both to drive personal growth and innovation.

Card Reflection: Unnatural Beauty

Shuffle your deck and lay out four cards, with the first card sitting on its own above cards two, three, and four.

1. What is a perceived imperfection in something "unnatural"?

2. What past experiences, beliefs, or influences contribute to this point of view?

3. What is the benefit of holding this imperfection?

4. Is there an opportunity to transmute this imperfection for learning, growth, or evolution and come back to "neutral?"

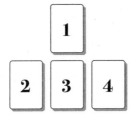

Affirmation

I embrace the diversity and complexity of my being.

THE DECANS OF GEMINI

Out there, someone needs to hear your words.
Out there, someone needs to see your art displayed.
Out there, someone's transformation depends on your
skills and knowledge.

Communication facilitates connection.
Connection facilitates change.
The change that someone out there
Could be waiting for.

Will you follow the call to be that person?
That person who offers themselves to another
Their art
Their wisdom
Their guidance
In a way only they can?

Someone needs your words.
Someone needs your music.
Someone needs your song.
Someone needs your light.
Someone needs to seek your darkness.

Your transformation
Can be the spark
Of magic
Someone needs
To find
The spark
Of
Magic
Within
Themselves

The spark that fuels the evolution of our world.

GEMINI I: YOUR WORDS WILL SET YOU FREE

Eight of Swords as Jupiter in Gemini

How we communicate with ourselves and others can propel us toward or away from the life we desire. All thoughts are valid, but not all thoughts can stay. Our needs are valid but should be communicated clearly and carefully and tempered by acknowledging the needs of others. We can advocate for a side to understand the contours of our perspective. Learning how to blend different communication styles increases our capacity to relate to others and heal ourselves.

REDIRECTING AUTOMATIC NEGATIVE THOUGHTS

Automatic Negative Thoughts (ANTs), as coined by psychiatrist, neuroscientist, and author Dr. Daniel Amen, are those uninvited guests that often linger in our minds, casting a shadow over our potential. They tell us we aren't good enough, that we can't achieve our goals, or that everything is going wrong. They are automatic because they seem to pop up without our control or even our awareness.

Dr. Amen has dedicated much of his work to understanding the brain's intricacies and how it influences our thoughts and behaviors. His research has led him to identify these ANTs and their impact on our mental health and overall well-being.

When someone repeatedly thinks and repeats fearful thoughts, it sets off a chain of events in the brain and nervous system, activating the amygdala and initiating the fight-or-flight response. This leads to a release of stress hormones like cortisol and adrenaline into the bloodstream. While beneficial in acute situations, when fearful thoughts are repeated over time, this cycle of fear can have detrimental long-term effects on the body and contribute to anxiety disorders.

According to Dr. Amen, we all have ANTs, and they usually fall into one of nine categories: All-or-Nothing Thinking, Always Thinking, Focusing on the Negative, Fortune Telling, Mind Reading, Thinking with Your Feelings, Guilt Beating, Labeling, and Blame. Recognizing these types of ANTs is the first step in learning how to combat them.

The Parable of the Man at Bethesda, a story Jesus taught to illustrate the healing power of mindset and words, and Louise Hay's influential book *You Can Heal Your Life*, both agree with Dr. Amen's work and further emphasize the transformative power of affirmations as a tool for redirecting ANTs. Through the power of affirmations, we can shift the mental patterns underlying disease in the body.

Understanding the science behind fear-based thinking helps us recognize the profound impact it has on our bodies. By becoming aware of our thought patterns and actively working to reframe fearful thoughts, we can interrupt this cycle and lessen the long-term effects on our physical and mental well-being. Techniques such as cognitive-behavioral therapy, mindfulness, and meditation have been shown to be effective in rewiring the brain and reducing anxiety by promoting more positive and adaptive thought patterns.

By acknowledging and challenging our ANTs, replacing them with positive, empowering thoughts, and practicing mindfulness, we can start to control our ANTs instead of letting them control us.

Our thoughts and words are key to our healing. The world we live in today was formed by the words we spoke yesterday. And the world we want to live in five years from now begins with the words we think and speak today.

Card Reflection: Cultivating a Growth Mindset

Shuffle your deck and lay out six cards, with cards two through six in one line, and card one sitting above card three.

1. What is your current mindset and beliefs?
2. What do you feel like you cannot do?

3. Why do you feel like you cannot do it?

4. No matter how small, what do you feel like you can do?

5. What support should you request?

6. What next step should you take?

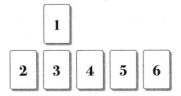

Affirmation

I embrace change and choose to see challenges as opportunities to make a choice.

HEALING WITH MERCURY: DIFFICULT CONVERSATIONS

Mercury, as the archetype of communication, is an essential aspect of managing difficult conversations. Its influence reminds us to choose our words carefully, ensuring clarity and precision in our expression. Like Mercury's duality, we should be adaptable and flexible, willing to consider different perspectives and find common ground.

For instance, when discussing political differences, employing effective communication methods inspired by Mercury can lead to a respectful exchange of ideas, fostering understanding even amidst disagreement. Similarly, when navigating conversations about death or money, Mercury's energy encourages us to approach these sensitive topics with compassion, empathy, and an openness to dialogue.

Handling difficult conversations also requires a deep understanding of psychology and emotional intelligence. It entails recognizing and managing our own emotions and reactions, staying grounded, and avoiding personal attacks or defensiveness. By displaying emotional intelligence, we can respond thoughtfully and constructively, encouraging a productive exchange of ideas.

Many people would rather avoid difficult conversations because it's easier or they don't have the tools to handle them. Choosing avoidance, however, can have detrimental effects on our mental well-being. When we avoid challenging conversations, we often resort to people-pleasing, sacrificing our own needs and values to maintain an illusion of harmony. This pattern can lead to long-term negative impacts on our mental health, such as increased stress, anxiety, and a sense of disconnection from ourselves.

Exercise: Role-Playing a Difficult Conversation with Mercury

In tarot, Mercury is often represented by the Magician. Using the Magician card as a partner or observer, name the issue you are having and the person you have the issue with. If it is a group of people, just choose one person to begin. Start the role play by acknowledging your own emotions and fears surrounding the conversation, practicing self-compassion throughout the process. Clarify your intention as one to build bridges, find solutions, and move forward. Name your desired outcomes and identify any potential triggers that may arise.

Take a moment to pause and actively listen to your inner thoughts through a free-writing journaling exercise. Write about what the other person may say, validating the other person's perspective. If there are places where it is difficult to validate, keep processing until you can find a way to see both sides. State your ideal outcome and ask Mercury to give you a spirit of empathy, in a way that fosters compassion and connection, even if that connection is a mutual decision to step away from the relationship for a period.

When you decide to have the difficult conversation, remember, it's okay to take breaks if needed. Take moments for self-care, grounding exercises, or speaking with a trusted friend or therapist for support and guidance. Lastly, reflect on the growth and empowerment that comes from engaging in difficult conversations, as they provide opportunities for personal development, improved relationships, and enhanced mental well-being.

Card Reflection: Preparing for a Difficult Conversation

Shuffle your deck and lay out ten cards according to the spread below.

1. What is the issue?
2. Who do you have the issue with?
3. Name the issue. Begin with, "I feel . . ."
4. Honor your role in contributing to the issue.
5. State the ideal outcome you would like to achieve.
6. Potential reactions after you invite a response.
7. How can you be curious about these reactions?
8. What questions can you ask to learn more about these potential reactions?
9. Timing of conversation?
10. Final piece of advice from your guides?

Affirmation

I am proud of myself for having the courage to engage in this difficult conversation knowing that it is a powerful step toward personal growth and stronger relationships.

GEMINI II: EMBRACE THE DARK NIGHT

Nine of Swords as Mars in Gemini

We have seasons of unraveling. During these times, we are invited to embrace change—to allow the life we lived to become one of the past. We allow ourselves to let go of old forms and be birthed into a form anew. This can be scary. You can feel lost. But remember that the night will not be dark forever. Sunrise is on its way. And with the light comes an emergence of the truth of who you evolved to become.

ALIGN BELIEF TO DESIRED ACTION WITH THE KNIGHT OF SWORDS

During our dark nights, all we can focus on is how our lives are falling apart. But think too of the skills and opportunities gained in the dark. Seeds communicate with the darkness of the soil to receive the nutrients necessary for them to take root. A baby gestates in the darkness in the mother's womb before it can be ready to sustain life on its own. Bioluminescent fish sustain life in the dark. And even for humans, the cycles of dark and light help us regulate our circadian rhythms.

Dark nights are just part of life. They come. They stay. And they will pass.

The symbolism of the Knight of Swords helps you reframe incongruent beliefs into beliefs with power by challenging the assumptions and words that are moving you in a direction different than the direction you want to go in.

Exercise: Knight of Swords Tarot Meditation

Settle into a comfortable position, close your eyes, and take a few deep breaths. Allow your body and mind to relax, fully present in this moment.

Take a moment to set your intention for this meditation. State your desire to identify and reframe incongruent beliefs that are not aligned to the life you want to create. Examining our beliefs and the words that arise from our beliefs requires consciousness of our energy in the present moment. Take this time to align your mental energy with your emotional energy to speak words of creation and expectancy.

Visualize the image of the Knight of Swords tarot card in your mind's eye. See the knight, strong and determined, holding a sword aloft with clarity and decisiveness. Take a moment to absorb the energy and symbolism of this card—the embodiment of courage, intellectual prowess, and swift action.

Bring your awareness to your current beliefs and attitudes. Observe the thoughts and patterns that arise within you. What scripts do you have most often running in your head? Which phrases? Are these mental scripts and spoken words aligned to the life you want to create? Explore these beliefs with curiosity and openness.

Card Reflection: Reorienting Limiting Beliefs with the Knight of Swords

Take out a journal or a piece of paper and pen.

1. Write down the beliefs that you have identified.

2. How do these beliefs manifest in your daily life?

3. Where do they need to shift so that you may lead the life you want to lead?

Now, imagine yourself as the Knight of Swords. Visualize yourself wielding the sword of clarity and determination, ready to use the sword of your mental energy to cut and revise the beliefs that have expressed as words taking you away, instead of toward, the life you want to create. With each swing of the sword, feel these beliefs being released and replaced with beliefs that power you toward the life of your dreams.

Shift your focus to the empowering beliefs that you wish to cultivate within yourself.

- What beliefs and corresponding words can you put on repeat to rewire the limiting ones? When and how will you create a routine or ritual that will rewire the brain to imprint these words on your soul?

Visualize these new beliefs taking root within you, bringing confidence, resilience, and a deep sense of purpose. For example, turn, "I am too old to get the proper education" into "Age is just a number. I can go back to school whenever I want."

Affirmation

I align thought with word with action and allow the flow of life to guide me toward my desired experiences.

GEMINI III: FINDING AND SURRENDERING CONTROL

Ten of Swords as Sun in Gemini

When we feel lost, we often look for external solutions instead of internal solutions. Once we can identify the connection to the Source that exists within our selves, then we are able to form meaningful connections that bring us into the next chapter of our stories.

FINDING YOUR LOCUS OF CONTROL

In high-stress environments, every day can feel like a dark night of the soul. You may find yourself plagued by anxious, racing thoughts due to the relentless pace and intense demands of your work. These anxious thoughts can lead you into hating your job and doing everything but the work you've signed up for. One method that can prove beneficial is to periodically reframe your experiences to focus more on what's within your capability, rather than what's beyond your reach. This concept is often referred to as operating within your "locus of control."

Your internal locus of control signifies your ability to control the consequences of your actions. On the other hand, an external locus of control means recognizing that the outcomes of your actions are sometimes beyond your control.

Harnessing your internal locus of control can lead to improved academic achievement, better interpersonal relationships, enhanced learning abilities, increased curiosity, motivation to exercise, and resistance to addiction. It can even contribute to lower risks of hypertension and heart attacks.

An internal locus of control empowers you to accept that some circumstances simply are what they are and are beyond your influence. This acceptance can foster a nonreactive attitude toward environments that are beyond change and illuminate opportunities for collaboration, leading to a sense of peace despite the external chaos present in your life.

Exercise: Finding Your Locus of Control

To operate effectively within your locus of control, begin by pinpointing the elements that fall within your *zone* of influence. These could include your thoughts, actions, and how you respond to various situations. Rather than expending energy *mulling over* aspects beyond your control, channel that energy into proactive measures and fostering positive shifts in areas where you hold *sway*. For instance, instead of allowing stress about unpredictable weather to consume you, concentrate on how you can adjust your plans to suit any given climate. This shift in focus is not only empowering but also helps you navigate life with greater ease and confidence.

Card Reflection: From Chance to Choice

Shuffle your deck and lay out six cards according to the spread below.

1. What are you anxious about? We all get anxious. Name it.

2. What do you have control over?

3. What do you not have control over?

4. What do you need to keep?

5. What do you need to release?

6. What next step should you take?

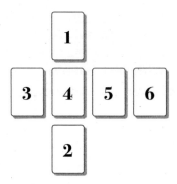

Affirmation

I know the difference between what I can and cannot change. The only person I can control is myself. I take responsibility for my actions and allow the Universe to decide when or if it will intervene.

THE DECANS OF CANCER

Divine Mother
As we return to the
Watery womb
From which we were
Birthed
We surrender to the
Cycles
We connect
to the Mother
We connect
With our ancestors
We take the energy
of what was
and
Combine with the energy
of what is
To transmute past into present
and present into future—
A future
inspired by
the depths
of emotion
existing in the ocean
of our hearts.
We heal from the outside in
But also the inside out.

CANCER I: HEALING PAST WITH PRESENT

Two of Cups as Venus in Cancer

Our internal landscapes are composed of areas familiar to us, and territories yet unexplored. By devoting time to understand our past, we can determine what we wish to retain, what we aim to let go, and what aspects require further inquiry. This empowers us to shape a life that aligns with our profound soul yearnings and that is guided by the Universe's callings.

SPEAKING WITH THE ANCESTORS

In the Thema Mundi, the classic birth chart of the Universe, the first decan of Cancer is on the Ascendant as the beginning of the zodiac. It symbolizes inception and the wise feminine energy—the concealed, mysterious force that can be felt but not seen. Light arises from the dark. The first decan of Cancer encourages us to reconnect with the parts of us that remain in the shadows—our ancestral links that connect us to the story of humanity. For only through acknowledging and comprehending these ties can we discern what we wish to keep, discard, or revise, as we continue to write our part of the human story.

Our introduction to Planet Earth begins with the personal histories of our biological parents—and their biological parents—that begin at conception. The body that hosts us in its womb and brings us forth into the world imprints us with a unique software (our past, our energy, and so on) that is subsequently transferred into our beings. To truly understand ourselves, we need to grasp the origin of this metaphorical software and decide the mindsets and actions that we want to continue with us into the future.

When we delve into our lineage, our past, and the histories of others, we can create a more resilient and just world for all. We are not owners; we are mere custodians of a physical form traveling through space-time. What happens now affects what happens in this life and the lives to come. And even if you don't subscribe to that idea, I think most people would reasonably agree that we want to leave our planet in at least the same, if not more conscious state, than when we encountered it.

Reflecting on our lineage compels us to think about legacy, tradition, and patterns that can be revised or replaced. Encountering the realities of our lineage provides us with space to heal our relationships with ourselves, others, and our forebears. When we meet our past with honor, understanding, and acceptance rather than shame, disgust, and regret, we gain a more dynamic understanding of who we are in the present moment. We see what we can do to heal ourselves and contribute to the healing of the world and its consciousness.

Exercise: Connecting with Your Ancestors

How can you uncover the mysteries of your biological ancestry? What legacies does your body carry? How did your birth story shape you? How can you delve deeper into understanding yourself? You might consider exploring options such as DNA testing, genealogy websites, Emotional Freedom Techniques (EFT), or seeking a natal chart consultation from an astrologer you trust. If you would like to connect with those who have come before you more generally, consider creating a dedicated ancestor altar or discover a sacred space where you can honor and connect with your ancestors regularly.

Note: Please be aware that delving into your ancestral past can unearth unexpected feelings. For instance, if you were adopted, you might feel as though you lack a tangible lineage to connect with. The same may be true for those who have experienced parental abuse. However, if you choose to embark on this journey, embrace everything you discover with integrity and compassion. The past is not just something to be studied—it's also a wellspring of lessons to draw from.

Card Reflection: Ancestors

Shuffle your deck and lay out six cards according to the spread below.

1. What is your ancestry?
2. What are some helpful ways your ancestors have impacted your life?
3. What are some unhelpful ways your ancestors have impacted your life?
4. What is the present state of your ancestral connection?
5. Are there any messages from the ancestors about the future of your connection?
6. What next steps should you take?

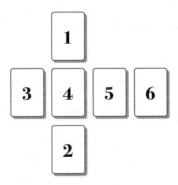

Affirmation

I partner with my past to create my present.

CONNECTING PAST AND PRESENT LIVES

Rebecca Campbell's book, *Rise Sister Rise*, was a significant catalyst in my burnout healing journey. It introduced me to the concept of the Akashic Records, a term I had never come across before. With curiosity, I decided to immerse myself in Campbell's meditation and consequently delve into Brian Weiss's book, *Many Lives, Many Masters*. It was a deep dive into my psyche, a pause, and an introspective journey to decipher the subconscious and unconscious narratives shaping my life.

The Akashic Records, often portrayed as a cosmic library or a universal knowledge reservoir, are believed to hold the collective consciousness and experiences of all souls across time. In spiritual disciplines, accessing these records can offer insights, guidance, and soul-level healing. By connecting with this divine information source, one can obtain a deeper understanding of their life purpose, karmic cycles, and spiritual progression.

We each harbor multiple selves working in harmony. These selves have been defined differently by various philosophies: Saved and unsaved. The Divine Self and the False Self. The id, ego, and superego. Regardless of the terminology, the underlying principle remains the same: there is who we are, who we want to be, and who we pretend to be. Healing occurs when our true self and our aspirations get into agreement. However, this agreement is easier said than achieved. Sometimes, who we aspire to be isn't in sync with our inherent nature or the Universe's design for us. Just like dissonance in music is unstable and resolved through shifting tones, the dissonance between who we were created to be and who we are, if held for a length of time, can contribute to the state of too much repair and not enough creation we know to be burnout.

This idea is also embodied in the concept of karma, which has its origin in Indian religions, and its role in the cycle of birth and death. Karma encapsulates the law of cause and effect. It proposes that every action—physical, mental, or verbal—generates repercussions that mold our present and future experiences. This understanding of karma extends beyond a single lifetime, as it's believed that the soul reincarnates multiple times until it attains liberation (moksha).

Engaging with past lives and the Akashic Records can help navigate these issues safely through symbolism and storytelling. Without undertaking this inner work, we often unknowingly perpetuate subconscious narratives of old patterns and lives inherited from our ancestors and lineage—whether from this life or previous ones—that we do not wish to keep in this life.

Working within the Akashic Records, the goal is to identify, mend, and heal old karmic patterns. It is similar to how an acupuncturist uses needles to shift energy, or how a chiropractor employs adjustments to move energy around the body so who we were designed to be is in agreement with who we want to be.

Exercise: Using Willow Energy to Connect with the Akashic Records

Across cultures and spiritual traditions, the willow tree holds profound symbolism. Revered for its ethereal beauty and serene presence, it is often associated with healing, intuition, and the realm of dreams. In ancient Celtic folklore, the willow tree was seen as a gateway to the Otherworld, a place where spirits and divine wisdom resided. This concept aligns with the idea of tapping into the Akashic Records, a cosmic source of knowledge and insight.

During meditation, the symbolism of the willow tree can be used to facilitate connection with the Akashic Records. Visualize yourself sitting under a majestic willow tree, its graceful branches flowing around you like a protective canopy. Envision the tree as a conduit between the earthly realm and the spiritual realm, allowing you to access the vast wisdom stored within the Akashic Records. Immerse yourself in the tree's energy, feeling its calming presence and deep-rooted connection to the Earth.

To enhance your connection with the Akashic Records, focus on the qualities associated with the willow tree during your meditation. Embrace the tree's flexibility and adaptability, allowing yourself to be open and receptive to the messages and insights that come through. Let go of any resistance or preconceived notions, surrendering to the flow of wisdom from the Records. Trust your intuition and the guidance that arises during this sacred practice.

It is important to approach the use of the willow tree as a tool to access the Akashic Records with reverence and respect. Before beginning your meditation, set a clear intention to connect with the Records and seek authentic, soul-aligned knowledge. Remember that the willow tree is a symbol and representation of this connection; it is the energy and intention you bring to the practice that ultimately facilitates the connection.

Card Reflection: Free-Writing after a Visit to the Akashic Records

During your reading, shuffle the tarot cards while focusing on your connection with the Akashic Records. Draw one card for each position, laying them side by side, and interpret their meanings in relation to your question or inquiry. Trust your intuition and allow the messages from the cards and the Akashic Records to guide you toward greater self-awareness, healing, and spiritual growth.

1. **Past Life Energies:** This card indicates influences from past lives affecting your current journey. Contemplate how these energies impact your present.

2. **Soul Lesson:** This card unveils the main lesson your soul aims to grasp in this life. Reflect on how this lesson can aid your spiritual development.

3. **Karmic Patterns:** This card underlines recurring themes or karmic patterns in your life. Ponder how these patterns can steer you toward personal growth and healing.

4. **Divine Guidance:** This card signifies support and guidance from higher realms and spiritual guides. Heed any messages or insights as they provide wisdom and direction.

5. **Next Step:** This card suggests actions that align with your soul's purpose and highest good. Think about how you can put these steps into action to progress on your spiritual path.

Affirmation

The exploration of my past lives is a sacred journey that connects me to the vastness of the Universe and the eternal nature of my soul.

CANCER II: LAUGHTER AS MEDICINE

Three of Cups as Mercury in Cancer
Laughter ignites the soul's innate healing power.

MAKE TIME TO LAUGH

Laughter is a powerful form of healing and nourishing the soul. It activates the parasympathetic nervous system, relaxing our bodies and nourishing our soul by swapping cortisol for dopamine, oxytocin, and endorphins. It's been found that laughter positively affects immune function, cardiovascular health, and even pain tolerance. Additionally, laughing with others creates a sense of belonging and enhances relationships. Laughter can spark joy, elevate moods, and foster a positive life perspective.

When I was a high school math teacher working in Title I schools, stress was a constant companion. Tasked with solving issues of poverty, malnutrition, and resource scarcity while teaching students two or more grade levels, sometimes four or five grade levels in math, we had to persuade them of math's importance amidst unmet safety and security needs. As a team of novice teachers, we were thrust into challenging situations: we knew how to teach math but did not know how to work with all the other social, economic, and emotional needs coming our way.

Learning as we went was our only option, and teamwork was crucial. I was put on a team of people from across the country, with all sorts of backgrounds, and because we were there to focus on the children, any differences needed to be resolved, genuinely and with a sense of expediency. And so, we learned to communicate and forgive quickly, with conflicts always ending in laughter.

Despite our diverse backgrounds and biases, we found unity in shared laughter. Post-school venting sessions in each other's classrooms often dissolved into laughter. We found humor in our predicament, laughing at the stress and irony. Laughter became our healing balm, our shared self-care ritual that kept us from crumbling. This collaborative practice helped us be our best selves as teachers and navigate our challenging environment.

Exercise: Healing with Laughter

Embracing laughter as a form of self-care can boost your mental health, build a positive outlook, and help you feel more energized throughout the day. Here are some ways you can incorporate more laughter into your day.

- **Start Your Day with a Smile:** Begin each morning by setting an intention to find humor and joy in the day ahead. As you wake up, smile at yourself in the mirror and remind yourself of the power of laughter.

- **Surround Yourself with Comedy:** Seek out respectful, affirming, funny content that resonates with you. Follow comedians on social media, subscribe to a humor podcast, or find a movie or TV show that brings a smile to your face. Dedicate a few minutes each day to enjoy these comedic moments.

- **Find Humor in Everyday Situations:** Train your mind to spot the humorous side of life's situations. Look for the irony, absurdity, or unexpected twists in daily encounters. Practice reframing challenges as opportunities for laughter and growth.

- **Share Laughter with Others:** Connect with people who have a great sense of humor. Engage in lighthearted conversations, share funny anecdotes, or participate in activities that bring out the laughter in you and those around you.

- **Laughter Breaks:** Take short breaks throughout the day to engage in laughter exercises. Watch a funny video clip, read jokes, or swap humorous stories with a colleague or a friend. These breaks can refresh your mind, increase productivity, and release stress.

Card Reflection: On Laughter

Shuffle your deck and lay out four cards side by side.

1. When you laugh, how does it make you feel?
2. Do you want more or less of this feeling?
3. Where can you find what you desire?
4. What next step should you take?

Affirmation

I give myself permission to laugh with my entire being, genuinely, while making connections with others.

FINDING HUMOR IN IRONY WITH THE CHARIOT AND THE HIGH PRIESTESS

Exercise: Observing and Appreciating Irony in the Tarot

Irony, a tool that reveals unexpected outcomes and contradictions, often sparks humor and insight. Irony comes from close observation of interesting differences between expected and unexpected results that offer wisdom through laughter. Through irony, we can find humor in even tough situations, lightening our mood and expanding our view. The Chariot and the High Priestess can help us understand and appreciate this ironic humor.

The Chariot card symbolizes determination, control, and victory. It represents the drive to conquer, to push forward against all odds. But the traditional image of the Chariot is ironic—is it moving forward or staying still? Something that looks so glorious, but what if it's really an image of someone stuck in place? This kind of thinking is an example of situational irony—when reality contradicts our expectations. Roaring laughter may not result, maybe just a smile. When seen through an ironic perspective, the Chariot reminds us to find humor in such situations, to laugh at the absurdity of life's symbols. It teaches us that sometimes, the Universe has a sense of humor too, throwing a wrench into our carefully laid plans and inviting us to take a breather, to laugh, and to find joy in the journey, obstacles and all.

On the other hand, the High Priestess card embodies intuition, mystery, and the subconscious mind. She is the guardian of secrets and the holder of deep wisdom. Now, consider the verbal irony when the High Priestess, known for her profound insights, says something seemingly simple or mundane that carries a deeper, often humorous, meaning. This is the essence of verbal irony—where words express something contrary to truth or someone says the opposite of what they mean, often for comedic effect. The High Priestess encourages us to listen beyond the words, to appreciate the wit and wisdom hidden in ironic statements, and to find humor in the unexpected depths of everyday conversations.

In the dance of life, the Chariot and the High Priestess invite us to find humor in irony, to laugh at the unexpected, and to cherish the surprises along the way. They remind us that life isn't always about charging full speed ahead or delving into the depths of mystery. Sometimes, it's about enjoying a hearty laugh when the Universe goes left and we go right.

Card Reflection: Noticing Irony and Humor in Everyday Life

Shuffle your deck and lay out six cards according to the spread below.

1. **The Situation:** What was the situation where you observed irony? Can you identify the circumstances leading up to this ironic event?

2. **Expected Outcome:** What did you initially expect to happen in this situation? Can you symbolize your expectations?

3. **Actual Outcome:** What was the actual, ironic outcome? Can you shed light on how the reality contradicted your expectations?

4. **Personal Impact:** How did this instance of irony affect you personally? Did it bring about any changes in your feelings, thoughts, or perceptions?

5. **Lessons Learned:** What lessons or insights did you gain from this ironic event? Can you identify what you learned from this experience and how it contributed to your personal growth?

6. Next step?

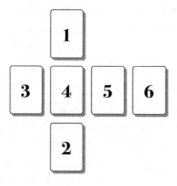

Affirmation

I find irony and humor in challenging situations, lightening my spirit and bringing joy to my journey.

FRIENDSHIP HEALING WITH THE QUEEN OF CUPS

The Queen of Cups is an empathetic companion, always ready to lend a listening ear and offer unwavering support. She creates safe spaces for others to express their feelings and intuitively understands unspoken needs. See her as your ally, bringing emotional stability and encouragement to your life.

A Tarot Meditation: Healing through Friendship with the Queen of Cups

Sit comfortably and close your eyes. Take a deep breath in, hold it for a moment, then exhale slowly. As you breathe in and out, imagine yourself being surrounded by a calming, healing energy. Picture the Queen of Cups, a tarot figure embodying emotional intelligence, compassion, and nurturing energy.

In your mind's eye, see the Queen holding a golden chalice overflowing with water. The chalice signifies her ability to hold space for others' emotions, while the water represents her limitless capacity for love and understanding. Feel her healing presence as she brings comfort to those around her.

Now, imagine the Queen of Cups infusing your friendships with her positive qualities. She sees the good in everyone and encourages you to express your true emotions. Picture her beside you, offering solace and support in times of need.

The Queen also understands the healing power of laughter. She finds joy in challenging circumstances and encourages you to approach life with a sense of humor. Visualize her light-heartedness, reminding you not to take life too seriously and to find common ground through humor.

Take a deep breath in, picturing a warm, golden light flowing through your body as you exhale. This light represents the joyous energy of the Queen of Cups, attracting positive friendships and experiences to your life.

Next, silently or aloud, repeat these affirmations:

1. I am open to friendships filled with laughter and joy.

2. Laughter and friendship come naturally to me.

3. I attract supportive friends into my life.

4. My life is rich with laughter and meaningful connections.

5. I find joy in every moment.

Continue to breathe deeply, letting the energy of these affirmations resonate within you. Feel gratitude for the abundance of friendship and laughter manifesting in your life.

When you're ready, gently bring your awareness back to the present. Open your eyes slowly, carrying the warmth and comfort of this meditation with you throughout your day. Remember, the Queen of Cups guides you toward deep connections and joyful experiences. Embrace the power of friendship and laughter, knowing they can heal and transform your life.

Affirmation

I choose to surround myself with friends who uplift, inspire, and bring out the best in me, creating a circle of joy and laughter.

CANCER III: BIRTHING YOUR DREAMS

Four of Cups as Moon in Cancer

Experience your emotions, but don't become your emotions. When it becomes challenging to navigate these emotions, music can communicate feelings and thoughts that words fail to express. After all, we are born of sound, and it is this very sound that can guide us through life when we find ourselves stuck.

GROUNDING THE DREAM

Sometimes we love living in the dream. From star seeds, to aliens, to wishing and hoping for a better world in the future, dreams propel us, but sometimes keep us stuck in a virtual reality world of our own creation. Grounding our dreams through inspired action is one way we can connect heaven with earth through the heart portal and be the change we wish to see in the world.

This can be difficult, however, when we haven't processed and healed our traumas. Dissociation is one way unprocessed or unhealed trauma manifests in the body. Dissociation is a complex psychological phenomenon that involves a disconnection between your thoughts, feelings, memories, and sense of identity. It can be a response to overwhelming or traumatic experiences. Like a defense mechanism protecting you from future pain or a coping mechanism that arises from overwhelming experiences.

The effects of dissociation can profoundly affect your life. Common symptoms of dissociation include feeling detached from our bodies and surroundings, a sense that the world is not as it should be, memory loss, shifting identities, and difficulty experiencing or expressing emotions. Procrastination can even be a type of disassociation. Connecting the mind with physical reality is one way you can invite your body to reenter the three-dimensional realm and construct reality instead of merely imagining it.

Exercise: Connecting with the Earth

Grounding exercises are valuable tools that help individuals anchor themselves in the here and now, fostering a sense of stability and connection. This exercise explores various techniques to bring awareness to the present moment and gradually heal dissociation.

Engage your senses: Bring your attention to your senses one by one.

- **Sight**: Notice five things you can see. Focus on their colors, patterns, and movements.

- **Hearing**: Listen for four distinct sounds around you. Be present with each sound, whether it's distant or nearby.

- **Touch**: Identify three things you can physically touch. Feel their texture, temperature, and weight. Fully experience the sensation against your skin.

- **Smell**: Notice two scents in your surroundings. Breathe in deeply and try to identify the aromas present.

- **Taste**: Pay attention to one taste in your mouth. Take a moment to savor it fully.

Finally, activities such as music, cooking, gardening are wonderful ways to engage multiple senses and reconnect with the earth and its energies.

Remember, recovery from dissociation is a deeply personal journey that often requires professional support, self-care practices, and peer support.

Affirmation

With each breath, I anchor myself in the present moment, grounding my mind and body, inspired by my dreams, but ultimately getting up to act.

THE DECANS OF LEO

Divine Father
Above
Below
Within
Without
All around,
We come to you
In a spirit of generosity
Seeking Agreement
With You
With Ourselves
and with the People, Places, and Things
Around Us.
Make manifest the provision for our needs in a way sufficient
for this present moment.
Help us become the solution to our problems, and
Show us what problems don't need our solution.
Let us be a clear channel
For giving
For Receiving
For all that is for us.
For your light gives us life
And your light shines forever
and ever
and ever
And so it is.

LEO I: TURNING CONFLICT INTO COLLABORATION

Five of Wands as Saturn in Leo

Sometimes the best people for a role are the people we were just in conflict or competition with. When we collaborate with people who have different perspectives from us, we can check confirmation biases and create new solutions that may not have been available to us before.

WHEN RIVALS BECOME COLLABORATORS

When navigating the complexity of human relationships, we inevitably cross paths with individuals who challenge us. They may appear in our professional environments, during casual errands, or even infiltrate our safe havens. These individuals stir emotions within us, trigger discomfort, and often incite feelings of animosity or jealousy. The modern mantra propagated by social media memes advises us to distance ourselves, establish firm boundaries, and find solace within our comfort zones. Yet, this approach, while temporarily useful, if set in for the long term, deepens societal divisions. The path toward collective growth necessitates learning how to engage, understand, and collaborate with those we consider difficult. After all, the exchange of knowledge is a two-way street.

This concept can be hard to digest. Our instinctual reactions often lean toward tribalism—seeking refuge among those who mirror our thoughts, behaviors, and emotions. It requires a certain level of inner peace and security to view the "other" as a potential ally rather than an outsider. However, when we manage to bridge these divides and work in tandem with those we naturally conflict with, we unlock doors to new opportunities. This collaboration allows us to harness the power of diverse perspectives, leading to creations that surpass what we could achieve in isolation.

The power of such a strategy is beautifully illustrated in Pulitzer Prize–winning author Doris Kearns Goodwin's book, *Team of Rivals*. Goodwin chronicles how President Abraham Lincoln skillfully managed a cabinet filled with conflicting personalities and political factions. Through his leadership, he laid the groundwork for abolition and the end of the Civil War.

Exercise: Cultivating a Network of Rivals

Consider your friend lists. On your phone, on social media, in your address book. Do you have a mix of diverse perspectives? People whom you know you will come into conflict with to catalyze evolution. People who balance you out? People who will empathize and understand? People in the same positions as you? I once had a mentor tell me that everyone should have an upline, downline, and sideline. I agree with this advice and would add, an upline, downline, and sideline of someone from the "other side." An easy way to do this is to follow social media accounts that would "disrupt the algorithm." Often social media algorithms pair us with what they "think" we will like, not what we are liking in the present moment. Consider how you can transcend the echo chamber and seek sources, online, but also offline, that build the rich diversity of your network.

Card Reflection: Building a Team of Rivals

Shuffle your deck and lay out seven cards according to the spread below.

1. **Project or Activity:** Why is this team coming together?

2. **Team Foundation:** What are the core values and principles that hold your team together despite the rivalries?

3. **Rival Forces:** What are the differing viewpoints or rival elements within your team?

4. **Conflict Resolution:** What strategies can be used to manage conflict and harness it for growth within your team?

5. **Team Harmony:** How can you foster unity and cooperation within your team without stifling individuality?

6. **Team Growth:** What potential does your team have for growth and success by leveraging its diversity?

7. What next step should you take?

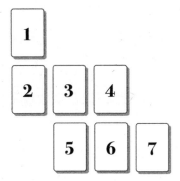

Affirmation

Competition and collaboration serve as powerful catalysts for creation. I compete and I collaborate as I create.

REWILDING THE SACRED MASCULINE WITH THE SUN

In many spiritual realms, there's a growing emphasis on the resurgence of the divine feminine, often portrayed as a counterpoint to the masculine. However, as we celebrate the ascension of the feminine, it's crucial to avoid becoming oppressors in our quest to overcome oppression. The aim should not be dominance, but rather choosing our desired polarity with the masculine or yang forces. This doesn't negate the necessity for reparations, apologies, or forgiveness—it simply means our vision should be one of intentional partnership. In the Chinese philosophy of yin and yang, it's not about one prevailing over the other, but the harmonious integration of both. As we shape the future, we need both yin and yang. We cannot polarize the spirit or genders. It's essential to foster a safe environment for healing during life phases. Ultimately, our goal should be reconciliation because we indeed are "better together."

Sophie Strand's "The Flowering Wand: Rewilding the Sacred Masculine" delves into the myths that have shaped our perception of masculinity. Her research reveals that masculinity wasn't always synonymous with hierarchy and dominance. Rather, it was associated with playfulness, mischief, and nature. By analyzing masculine figures in their historical context, she reimagines the narrative of Jesus as a Jewish teacher with nature-based and magical teachings—a wild Christianity whose roots spread throughout the ancient world. This contrasts sharply with the modern portrayal of Jesus—a figure detached from his natural ecosystem, making his teachings susceptible to manipulation. By reconnecting Jesus with his Jewish heritage, we see him as an activist—a revolutionary who defied the norm with innovative ideas to advance society.

Thus, when examining sacred masculine figures like Jesus and the interpretation of his teachings, we should ask ourselves: Does this interpretation honor the sacred texts of the Jewish people? Or has this teaching become so disconnected from its roots that it feels devoid of life, even when the words seem alive? Do we perceive Jesus as the Hierophant in the tarot, or do we see him as the Magician? I propose that Jesus is akin to the Magician and the planet Mercury—an intermediary between two realms—the visible and the invisible. They all embody the same archetypal concept of a person who can harness the fundamental elements of life—and bridge the connection between Heaven and Earth.

Exercise: Embracing the Sun

Free-write for five minutes on any thoughts, feelings, or physical sensations that come up when you read the following:

Reflecting on the celestial influence of the Sun in our astrological chart, we become aware of its pivotal role in shaping our personality and individuality. The Sun, as the energy-generating luminary in our solar system, symbolizes our core essence, vitality, and self-expression. Its placement in our chart reveals the balance between the divine masculine (Sun) and divine feminine (Moon) energies within us. It helps us understand how these energies interact and manifest in our day-to-day lives.

The Sun's position in different houses illuminates the areas where we yearn to express our true selves, assert our individuality, and shine brightly. When in a fire sign, it radiates with passion and creativity, while in an earth sign, it embodies practicality and stability. In an air sign, it reflects intellectual curiosity and sociability, and in a water sign, it signifies emotional depth and sensitivity.

This understanding allows us to embrace dualities within ourselves. We can recognize our strengths as well as vulnerabilities, and learn to assert ourselves confidently while honoring our receptive and nurturing side. This balance forms the foundation for a harmonious and complete sense of self, enabling us to navigate life's challenges with grace and resilience.

Cultivating this balance involves nurturing both active and receptive qualities within us. Engaging in activities that ignite our passions, assert our desires, and tap into our creative expression cultivates the divine masculine energy. On the other hand, embracing introspection, connecting with our emotions, and nurturing ourselves and others nourish the divine feminine energy.

By integrating the energies of the Sun and Moon within ourselves, we foster a profound sense of wholeness and balance. This integration allows us to lead more authentic and fulfilling lives, creating harmonious relationships with others and the world around us. The Sun's placement in our astrological chart serves as a constant reminder of the importance of balancing these energies to unlock our fullest potential. By working with the Sun to rewild the sacred masculine, we can truly thrive in our own unique light.

Card Reflection: Rewilding the Sacred Masculine

Shuffle your deck and lay out six cards according to the spread below.

1. **Sacred Masculine:** How is the sacred masculine energy currently manifesting in your life?

2. **Divine Feminine:** How is the divine feminine energy currently manifesting in your life?

3. **Balance:** What steps can you take to go with the flow of these energies within you?

4. **Hierophant vs. Magician:** How can you shift your perception of masculine figures between the Hierophant (authority figure) to the Magician (intermediary between realms)?

5. **Integration:** How can you integrate the energies of the Sun and Moon within yourself for a more profound sense of wholeness and balance?

6. What next step should you take?

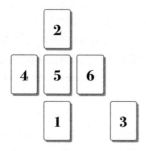

Affirmation

I am open to learning from the wisdom of both the Sun and Moon.

LOVE PEOPLE FOR WHO THEY ARE, NOT WHO YOU WISH THEM TO BE

In our society, many deeply rooted institutions embody the energy of masculinity. Often, we find ourselves on the outskirts or bear the pain from institutions we once trusted. These were places meant to provide solace and comfort.

For me, that institution was the church. During a time when I desperately needed support, I was cast aside because I didn't fit their template of what a "good Christian girl" looked like. I was labeled a sinner, deemed unworthy. Reacting defensively, I distanced myself completely from my faith. I renounced Jesus and adopted a stance of being "spiritual—not religious."

Sometimes, the most effective way to collaborate is by demonstrating our disagreement through our actions. We can choose to leave an organization that no longer aligns with our beliefs. It's not about promoting cancel culture, but rather about taking control of our situation. Departing due to philosophical differences comes from a place of self-respect and integrity. It's a statement that says, "These are my convictions—this institution does not align with them. . . I disagree on a fundamental level. . . I don't wish to disrupt those who find value in this space, so I will respectfully exit."

Closely relating to a dogmatic, authoritarian religion can lead to religious trauma syndrome (RTS). According to the Religious Trauma Institute, RTS is the "physical, emotional, or psychological response to religious beliefs, practices, or structures that overwhelm an individual's ability to cope and return to a sense of safety." Continued exposure to beliefs incongruent with love, tolerance, and acceptance can damage your nervous system over time, leaving lasting effects like PTSD, depression, emotional dysregulation, social dysfunction, intrusive thoughts, and more.

In the tarot, the Hierophant card can be particularly triggering for many, as it often reminds them of negative experiences with religious institutions. If you ever feel uneasy questioning an inherited belief system or disassociate during discussions about religious beliefs, it may indicate that these systems are rooted in trauma. If you feel trapped within a belief system, faced with punishment if you were to change your mind, or if those still within the system feel threatened by your departure, it suggests there may be unresolved trauma that needs healing or ties that need cutting. Not just for your own well-being, but also for theirs.

Sometimes, when people have time apart to reconsider who they are as individuals rather than who they are as a member of a group, in the future they can reconnect in community in a different way that honors the desires and needs of the other. Relationships can be, but do not have to be, all or nothing. Consider the variance of options that exist with the people in your life and act accordingly.

Exercise: Lavender as a Healing Partner for Religious Trauma

Lavender, a plant steeped in medicinal, spiritual, and cultural significance, has been a source of healing and serenity for centuries. Its roots trace back to the French monarchy, where it was an emblem of elegance and luxury, and it continues to be an iconic symbol of the region of Provence. The calming aura of lavender can be a powerful tool in your journey toward healing, particularly if you're working with RTS.

Start by finding a quiet, comfortable space where you won't be disturbed. You may choose to sit or lie down, whatever feels most comfortable for you. Close your eyes and take a few deep breaths, allowing your body and mind to relax.

Next, imagine yourself in a vast field of lavender in the heart of Provence. Picture the vibrant purple blooms stretching out as far as the eye can see, swaying gently in the breeze under the clear blue sky. The air is filled with the soothing scent of lavender, a fragrance that has been cherished for its calming properties.

As you inhale, imagine the healing energy of lavender filling your body, washing over you like a gentle wave. With every exhale, let go of any tension, pain, or negative emotions that you've been holding on to.

Now, recall any experiences with religious institutions that have caused you pain. Acknowledge these feelings without judgment and remind yourself that it's okay to feel this way. As you breathe in the calming energy of lavender, visualize it soothing these painful memories, replacing them with feelings of peace and acceptance.

As you continue to breathe in the soothing aroma of lavender, imagine yourself growing stronger with each breath. With every exhale, visualize any residual pain or trauma being released, leaving only peace and tranquility behind.

Slowly bring your awareness back to the present moment. Take a few more deep breaths, savoring the lingering scent of lavender. When you're ready, gently open your eyes.

Incorporating this lavender meditation into your daily routine can be a powerful tool in your healing journey. And remember, healing takes time. Be patient with yourself and trust in your resilience and strength.

Card Reflection: Reworking Mental Patterns

Reflect on the Hierophant card. What feelings or thoughts does it evoke within you? How can you take these emotions and rework your mental patterns around them through silencing the mind, breathing, or talking with a friend or professional? If you like, draw additional cards to continue to have a conversation with yourself around this card.

Affirmation

I have the power to choose my spiritual path and beliefs.

LEO II: VICTORY BEGINS AND ENDS WITH SERVICE

Six of Wands as Jupiter in Leo

Service is part of love. We are here to create and then to give. We can, however, only give what we have. We cannot give out of an empty cup. When we attempt to, our giving is conditional on what we receive in return. Service is not doing with the expectation of reciprocity. Service is doing because you want to, because it benefits both individual and collective.

SEEKING THE WIN-WIN THROUGH SERVICE TO OTHERS

In our societal narrative, there's often a binary division between winners and losers. We're conditioned to adopt a mindset where personal triumph is seen as coming at the expense of others: "If I rise, you must fall." This perspective seeps into various areas of our lives, from our chase for wealth and power to our social interactions and relationships. We measure and compare, suggesting that worthiness isn't inherent but dependent on physical, mental, or emotional traits.

This win-lose mindset is cultivated in our early years, starting with experiences in our education system. Instead of cultivating mutual respect, cooperation, and creativity, many schools encourage competition by grading students against their peers rather than assessing their objective knowledge of content. Many educators resist standards-based grading, resulting in inaccurate feedback on students' strengths and areas for improvement. Accepting that we all have strengths and areas for growth is crucial for creation. We can only thrive in creative partnerships when we recognize our strengths and weaknesses and collaborate with those whose skills complement ours. Complementarity fuels creativity, painting a vibrant technicolor world as opposed to a monochromatic existence bound by sameness.

Grading against established standards isn't about competition or supremacy; it's about harnessing our full human potential, knowing that we can all succeed, and understanding the steps necessary to attain mastery in a subject.

To foster a society where everyone can thrive, we need to shift from a competitive mindset to a collaborative one. This change involves acknowledging our needs and understanding their intersection with the needs of others. It's about developing our character, nurturing meaningful relationships, and creating agreements that reflect our mutual dependence. Adopting a win-win mindset demands empathy and bravery. It challenges the belief in scarcity, asserting that despite limited resources, there's more than enough for everyone if we work together with a sense of trust, intention, and shared direction.

A win-win mindset redefines success. It communicates that your success doesn't denote my failure; rather, it lays the groundwork for collective growth and prosperity.

Exercise: "It's Okay If I Don't Win"

In a world that often emphasizes winning, it can be hard to accept that we're not always going to be the first or the best at everything. But remember, it's perfectly okay not to be first. In fact, recognizing our weaknesses can be incredibly empowering. It helps us understand where we need support from others and how we can form meaningful and complementary relationships.

So, for today's journal exercise, let's take a deep, accepting look at ourselves.

Step 1: List Your Weaknesses. Begin by writing down a list of things that drain your energy or kill your joy. This is not an exercise in self-deprecation but rather a moment of honesty with yourself. These could be skills you're still developing or areas where you consistently feel challenged.

Step 2: Embrace Your List. Now, look at that list and embrace it. Instead of feeling ashamed or discouraged, understand that these are areas where you can learn more about or delegate. Write down next to each point, "I accept and love this part of me."

Step 3: Seek Complementarity. Reflect on how these weaknesses might guide you in seeking collaborators. For each point, write down the type of person or skill that could complement your weakness. For example, if you struggle with organization, you might seek someone who is naturally systematic and structured.

Step 4: Attracting the Right Relationships. Consider how being open and accepting about your weaknesses can attract the right relationships into your life. Write a few lines or paragraphs reflecting on this. How does acknowledging your weaknesses make you more approachable? How does it allow for more honest, fulfilling relationships?

Step 5: Celebrate Your Strengths. Finally, don't forget to celebrate what you are good at. Write down a list of your strengths and take a moment to appreciate them. Understand that just as you have weaknesses that others can complement, your strengths can also complement others' weaknesses.

Card Reflection: Embracing Both Strength and Weakness

Combine the Six of Wands with the Two of Cups. Consider the Two of Cups. This card symbolizes partnership, mutual respect, and balance. This card encourages you to embrace your weaknesses and strengths alike, recognizing that they make you who you are. Just as two cups can hold different liquids but are equally important, your strengths and weaknesses are different but equally valuable parts of you.

Compare this card to the Six of Wands. What does the Two of Cups have to say about the Six of Wands? What does the Six of Wands have to say about the Two of Cups? How can these perspectives be reconciled?

Affirmation

I am worthy because I am intrinsically worth it. My worth is not dependent on how others define my worth.

HEROES DON'T ALWAYS HAVE FOLLOWERS WITH THE SUN AND STRENGTH

In his book *The Hero with a Thousand Faces*, Joseph Campbell summarizes the monomyth of the "hero's journey" as one where a common person journeys out to encounter forces that support decisive victory. After victory, the hero returns home and returns the gift to his fellow man. There are trials, allies, and a metaphorical death and resurrection.

There are many examples of the monomyth in modern Hollywood. From *Star Wars* to *The Lion King* to *The Matrix*, we often misinterpret the common story about a person who finds their own success, their own strength, or arrives at some more enlightened state or righteousness. We look to social media likes and follows to determine how "influential" someone is. Because if they have a lot of followers, they must be doing something worth emulating, right? Sometimes yes and sometimes no. Sometimes, the most effective heroes, in fact, are focused on making an impact offline by being generous and offering their gifts to others. These heroes understand how to follow their creative muse—how to follow what lights their soul on fire—and how to discard what remains. For anything they're neutral about, they understand how to consult with advisers to put themselves back into their creative flow. When you're in the presence of a creative or generative person, you feel supported. Their energy field is tuned for generosity of spirit.

So many heroes in our world are winning in silence—the nurse working overnight shifts with sick patients, the teacher staying after hours to tutor students and write lesson plans, the business owner supporting the distribution of products to people they share their offering with. These heroes manage their egos to not fall into the trap of martyrdom. They know it's not about them—it's about being a portal for the creative force to flow through them and connect with the people they are designed to connect with.

Exercise: Power Together with the Sun and Strength

The Sun and Strength cards from the tarot deck offer powerful imagery for this exercise. The Sun represents joy, success, and celebration, while Strength symbolizes inner power, love, and patience. You can use these images to explore the concept of "power with" instead of "power over."

Step 1: Visualize the Sun. Imagine the warmth of the sun, its radiant light spreading in all directions, touching everything equally. The Sun doesn't dominate; it shares its energy generously. Write about a situation where you shared your power and influence generously, like the sun. How did it make you feel? How did it impact others?

Step 2: Embrace Your Strength. Now, picture the Strength card, showing a person taming a lion with love and patience. This is not about overpowering but about inner strength and understanding. Reflect on a time when you used your inner strength to handle a situation, not by exerting control but by demonstrating understanding and patience. What was the outcome?

Step 3: Imagine a "Power With" Scenario. Think about a recent interaction where you had the opportunity to exert "power over" someone else. How could you have turned that into a "power with" scenario? Write down what you could have done differently.

Step 4: Envision Future Scenarios. Finally, envision future scenarios where you can practice "power with" instead of "power over." What are some ways in which you can share your power generously and use your strength for understanding and patience?

This exercise is about recognizing and shifting your power dynamics. By practicing "power with," you foster an environment of shared influence and mutual growth.

Card Exercise: Message from the Sun and Strength

Draw one card. This is the message the Sun and Strength have for you. Continue the conversation with the cards if you would like to expand or seek clarification.

Affirmation

I connect with others through a spirit of generosity and authenticity.

SACRED ECONOMICS WITH THE KING OF WANDS

With rising inequality, increasing wealth inequality, shifts in power dynamics because of climate change, and political divisiveness, it can be easy to just disassociate and become jaded, feeling like there's nothing that you can do to change the world, or at least the world in your local community.

The B Corp movement, however, is one way people committed to creating conscious businesses to serve others and solve problems in their community—to participate in capitalism without being, well, capitalistic.

The B Corp movement creates a new kind of company that focuses on serving people and serving the planet, while still earning profit in exchange for the value they provide to society as they act in massive service to others. The B Corp is a business entity that places social benefits, the rights of workers, community, and the environment as criteria in addition to financial interests. It recognizes that "gross domestic product" should include noneconomic considerations. It embodies the idea that wealth does not just mean dollars and cents—it means the well-being of our people and our planet.

While capitalism, in its current form, is the root of many problems. When properly regulated by government, it can be a tremendous force for good by lifting people out of poverty, providing meaningful work, and embodying the idea that not everyone wants to be an entrepreneur or business owner. There are so many people who just want to show up to work, work flexible hours, and collect a paycheck that they can spend on the people, places, and things that light their soul on fire. And that's okay. In a world sometimes obsessed with entrepreneurship and innovation, B Corps remind us that there is also joy in finding work-life separation. All the better if we can show up to work in a place where we are not just collecting a paycheck but are part of a movement to provide for our people and our planet, while having fun doing it.

Tarot Card Meditation: Igniting Socially Conscious Change with the King of Wands

The King of Wands in a tarot deck represents charismatic leadership, vision, and creative energy. In the context of reshaping the current capitalist structure, the King of Wands symbolizes the potential for transformation and the application of these qualities to create a more equitable and just society.

As you contemplate the concept of benefit corporations, reflect on the possibilities they hold. How might this new form of capitalism transform our communities, our environment, and our collective well-being? Consider the ways in which you can support and champion benefit corporations, whether as a consumer, investor, or advocate.

Now, take a moment to set an intention. Journal about the changes you wish to see in the business world and how you can contribute to this transformation. Reflect on your own strengths, passions, and leadership qualities, and consider how you can align them with the principles of benefit corporations.

Carry the essence of the King of Wands and the concept of benefit corporations with you as you move through your day. Remember that you have the power to create positive change, both within yourself and in the world around you. Embrace your creativity, passion, and leadership, and let them guide you toward a future where capitalism serves the greater good.

Consider the brands and products that you buy.

1. What is the story behind each brand?
2. Are these benefit corporations?
3. How can you support more brands that are about people and the planet in addition (or instead of) profits?
4. If you are a business owner, have you considered becoming a benefit corporation? Why or why not? Visit www.bcorporation.net to learn more.

Card Reflection: Message from the King of Wands

Ask a question. Set the intention to the Universe that you would like the answer to this question to be in service of the greatest and highest good of all. Draw one card. Let this be the message from the King of Wands to you. Consider his insights and whether you would like to keep, ponder, or discard.

Affirmation

The success of my provision of goods and services in the transactional marketplace is measured not just by profit, but by societal and environmental impact.

LEO III: THE ART
OF PEACEFUL WAR

Seven of Wands as Mars in Leo

With every action, there is an equal and opposite reaction. By leveraging processes and systems set in place by our ancestors who lived through wars and famines, we can disrupt systems gracefully, in a way that does the least harm to ourselves and each other.

NOTHING TO PROVE

So often we live our lives defining our worth by what we do, how we perform, and what groups we are part of or not part of. This mentality leads us to exhaustion—to living according to the standards set by others. We look at people on social media and feel better or worse. We look at others in our industry and feel better or worse. We are in a constant comparison trap. And if we live in this mode instead of letting our own principles define us, we will always be at the mercy of others' approval. When we live a principle-centered life—centered in maximizing the skills, experiences, and desires that our souls inherited at birth—we become more effective, efficient, and joyful people with nothing to prove.

Principles are set from the inside out, from a place of inner knowing, security, and power. Principles are enduring and unchanging, even when the waves of life crash around us. In Stephen Covey's *The 7 Habits of Highly Effective People*, he describes a principle-centered life as one that lives proactively in a way that contributes to the values you determine in life.

We create our lives from the inside out. We write the scripts to our own stories. Healing and transformation begin with identifying the center from which your center flows—a center that is completely within the values that you have defined for yourself, not the values others have defined for you.

Exercise: Living a Principle-Centered Life

Living a principle-centered life requires you to reflect and identify the values that are most important to you. These are the core values that shape your decisions, actions, and interactions with others. Often, how we spend our resources—time, money, and energy—will reveal our values to you. You can then decide if you want to keep those values or decide to change how you spend your time or money on things that really matter to you.

Choose one principle that you want to live by. What habits, traits, mindsets, beliefs, and skills are evidence of this value? What will you see? What will you feel? What will you do? What will you not do?

Card Reflection: Core Values

Shuffle your deck and lay out five cards side by side.

1. What qualities do I admire in others?
2. What activities and experiences bring me joy?
3. When do I feel most authentic?
4. What core value do I want to embody in my relationships, work, and personal life?
5. What habits should I adopt that are aligned with this core value?

Repeat to brainstorm additional core values.

Affirmation

I live my life from my core values. I have nothing to prove.

STAY IN YOUR LANE AND RUN YOUR RACE

When I was in middle school, I loved track and field. My favorite event was the 400 meters (one lap around the track). The 400 is more than a sprint, so you must pace yourself. But it's also not long distance, so you must sprint at parts. One of the lessons I learned from this everyday experience was that the race was staggered to start. Some people were ahead to begin. Some people were behind. This was because the distance in lanes was different depending on whether you were in an inside lane or outside lane. This taught me that you could start out behind, but still come out first. All you had to do was stay in your lane and run your race. When you turned into that last 300, things came into vision.

The same principle applies in life. Our job is not to change minds to convince people to come into our lane. Our job is to walk in our purpose from our inner vision. When we seek external validation for work that should be inwardly validated, we end up giving our joy away to someone who doesn't even know us. Our work is to run our race, stay in our lane, and remember it's not about winning or losing in first, second, or third place. We all go across the finish line. And even if we don't, that's okay too. What matters is that we showed up and engaged our mind with our body. The only race we're really running is the one against ourselves.

Exercise: Building Intrinsic Motivation with the Lot of Spirit

When you are intrinsically motivated, you are more likely to experience a sense of fulfillment and satisfaction in your endeavors, as you are driven by personal growth and a genuine love for what you do. In astrology, this idea can be represented by the Lot of Spirit. The Lot of Spirit represents free will and the origin of that free will in consciousness. Often burnout can occur when we are doing the things that are not in agreement with the emanations of consciousness. It's like trying on shoes that look nice but are just not your size. Understanding your Lot of Spirit and its placement in your birth chart can reveal information about how we change our external environment by our own actions.

Locate your Lot of Spirit in your birth chart. Research and understand the energies of your Lot of Spirit. Consider its ruling planet, elements, modalities, and house placement. Reflect on your Lot, journal, and integrate your Lot of Spirit into daily living.

Card Reflection: Shifting Extrinsic Motivation to Intrinsic Motivation

Shuffle your deck and lay out six cards side by side.

1. What is an activity you are engaged in?
2. What external rewards result from your participation in this activity?
3. What internal rewards result from your participation in this activity?
4. What would happen if you only had internal rewards?
5. What would happen if you only had external rewards?
6. Is there a message from your intuition about potential next steps?

Affirmation

I am guided by my inner values and purpose. And while external rewards may result, they are not the focus.

THE DECANS OF VIRGO

Legacy is birthed
During life
Cultivated through the tending
The dedication to
And the restoration,
Of Earth
In synchrony
With the Universe.
We accept
The duty to give thanks
And recirculate
What we were given
Back to
that from
which it was
Formed.

VIRGO I: HARD WORK DOESN'T ALWAYS LOOK LIKE WORKING HARD

Eight of Pentacles as Sun in Virgo

Money is just energy. What you think about money will inform how money flows into your life. Caring about service and offering an energetic exchange that aligns with your life principles and personal values opens the portal for financial flow. This way you may serve as a channel for financial abundance—not just for yourself but for the collective.

AN UNCOMMON WAY TO WEALTH

As a burnt-out high school math teacher, I would periodically take a mental health day just to browse the used bookstores in Houston. Living paycheck to paycheck and working long hours, I knew I couldn't continue like this forever. I walked into the bookstore and asked the Universe to show me what book I needed to read. I walked up and down the aisles until a book caught my eye: a small green book with no title on the spine. I knew this was the one. I pulled it off the shelf to read the title: *An Uncommon Way to Wealth* by Victor D'Argent. I paid for the book, left the bookstore, and went home to read.

At a mere 61 pages, this book held wisdom about wealth that I had not previously encountered. It became a catalyst for my healing journey, challenging my beliefs and reshaping my understanding of what it truly means to be wealthy. The book emphasized that wealth is not just about how much money is in the bank account. Wealth is the natural consequence of uncommon behavior such as courage, humility, and curiosity. And when money flows in as financial abundance, it becomes less important.

Though written under a pseudonym, the author is believed to have been a prominent figure in the Parisian publishing industry. The book was discovered among private papers of a wealthy man and gifted to a publisher, who then shared it with the world.

Exercise: Opening the Root Chakra to Receive

Financial instability impacts the root chakra, creating imbalances and blockages that hinder our ability to attract financial abundance. This can manifest as a constant fear of lack, feelings of insecurity, or an inability to create sustainable financial foundations. It becomes crucial to address these imbalances and heal the root chakra to restore harmony in our financial lives.

To balance and heal the root chakra during financial difficulties, you can incorporate practices such as meditation, positive affirmations, and working with healing crystals like Red Jasper or Smoky Quartz. Begin by finding a quiet space, sitting comfortably, and focusing on your breath. Visualize a bright red energy spinning at the base of your spine, nourishing and revitalizing your root chakra.

While in this meditative state, repeat affirmations that resonate with you, such as:

- I embrace courage in the face of challenges, knowing that each obstacle is an opportunity for growth and transformation.

- I approach life with humility, recognizing that there is always more to learn and explore on my journey.

- I am curious about the world around me, seeking new experiences that expand my understanding and bring joy into my life.

- I trust in the process of manifestation and know that I have the power to attract into my life effortlessly.

- I set clear goals and intentions, taking inspired action daily to manifest my desires with ease and grace.

- I release any attachment to outcomes and surrender to the flow of the Universe, trusting that everything unfolds perfectly for my highest good.

Healing the root chakra and cultivating financial abundance is a gradual process. It requires patience, self-compassion, and consistent practice. By addressing the imbalances within the root chakra through meditation, affirmations, and working with supportive crystals, you can create a solid foundation for financial well-being and invite greater abundance into your life.

Card Reflection: Root Chakra

This five-card spread incorporates the properties of the root chakra and the significance of the number five in tarot readings. Shuffle your deck and lay out five cards side by side.

1. **Root Chakra:** What blockages or imbalances may be hindering your sense of security, stability, or groundedness?

2. **Courage:** Where can you find the courage to face any fears or challenges with moving through your energy blocks?

3. **Humility:** What constraints, limitations, or mistakes can you recognize and take ownership for, and how can this recognition pave the way for fresh relationships and avenues for learning?

4. **Curiosity:** What is one is one thing you can become curious about?

5. **Integration:** What next step should you take?

Affirmation

I trust that the Universe abundantly provides for my needs in the present moment.

HEALING THE MARTYR WITH MERCURY

In astrology, Mercury stands as the archetype of communication, intellect, and idea exchange, often bridging the gap between humans and gods. The concept of selfless service between those who have more and those who have less is frequently promoted in society as a mark of honor and virtue.

Numerous people hold on to the belief that by serving and giving to others, they demonstrate their humility and selflessness. They are always ready to lend a hand, perform kind acts, and make personal sacrifices in the name of "doing good." However, in this process, they may overlook the need to invest in themselves and fully harness their unique talents and abilities.

It's that idea—fill your cup first so you generate overflow to pour into others. When we start pouring into others from a half-full cup, we may unintentionally also share the parts of ourselves that have not yet been healed and integrated, if integration is necessary or desired.

Put another way, functioning from a position of martyrdom or seemingly sincere humility sends a signal to the Universe that we are seeking validation and accolades for our deeds. We are not giving from a generous heart or from a place of serious study or deeply lived experience; instead, we are giving in anticipation of a reward.

Rather than perpetually crucifying ourselves metaphorically, it's vital to contemplate how we can descend from selflessness and reconnect with the earth through our root chakra and introduce more selfishness into our lives. By doing this, we make room for others to contribute and enable them to assume their own roles and responsibilities.

This path begins with gratitude, acknowledging everything we have received from the Universe. This includes recognizing the tools we already have at our disposal, the clothes we wear, and the comforts of our homes and vehicles. If we find ourselves in a state of abundance, there's no need for guilt. Instead, we can channel this material energy back into the collective, sharing resources and spreading wealth.

It's important to realize that money is just energy, a tool to give and receive in a transactional marketplace in a way where everyone is fairly (generally) based on the economic principles of supply and demand. The real problem emerges when money is misused or purposefully used to inflict harm on others. This underscores that the issue lies with people, not the energy exchange itself.

By adopting a more nuanced view of selflessness, we can foster healthier dialogues with ourselves and others. We can respect our own needs while still discovering ways to elevate and assist those around us. Let's remember that true humility involves acknowledging and nurturing our own talents and abilities, thereby enabling us to serve others sincerely and with heartfelt empathy.

Exercise: Asking the Universe to Guide You to Your Purpose

If you want to be useful and feel like you haven't found your purpose, consider engaging courage, humility, and curiosity by trying some new things. Follow what lights your soul on fire and keep going until you feel like you've found it.

Research: Find industries, hobbies, and subjects that match your interests and skills. Find ways to use your skills and make a difference.

Networking: Meet experts in your interests. Find mentors or professionals to help you on your personal and professional path.

Try new things: Leave your comfort zone. Do things that test your limits and reveal your potential. Ask yourselves these questions to help you:

- What makes me happy and fulfilled?
- What are my natural abilities and strengths?
- What have people praised me for?
- Are there any skills I'm underusing?

Affirmation

I am a catalyst for positive contributions to the world because I invest what has been given to me in a way that yields a 100 percent return.

INVEST EVEN WHEN YOU THINK YOU HAVE NOTHING TO INVEST

We often underestimate the impact of investing in ourselves and others, especially when we believe we have nothing substantial to offer. But as the story of my own journey demonstrates, even in times of financial struggle and uncertainty, tithing and investing can create a transformative shift in our lives.

When I graduated from college during an economic depression, I faced the daunting challenge of limited job prospects and overwhelming student loan debt. I found myself relying on government assistance to make ends meet, feeling the weight of financial strain pressing down on me. During this struggle, I decided to attend a well-known megachurch in Houston, Texas, where I was introduced to the concept of tithing.

Tithing, the act of giving a portion of our income to support the work of the church or contribute to causes we believe in, initially seemed like an impossible task. With so little in my bank account, the idea of giving away *any* amount of money at that time felt daunting. Yet, I decided to start small, giving what I could—a mere $20.

Surprisingly, this shift in mindset began to change everything. By opening myself up to the flow of reciprocal financial energy, new opportunities started flowing into my life. I secured a part-time educational consulting position, created a program at our high school, and experienced a gradual improvement in my financial circumstances.

As money started flowing in, my initial reservations about tithing gradually faded away. Instead of feeling obligated to give a fixed percentage to a specific institution, I began following my intuition and giving to individuals and organizations that I felt called to support each week. The Universe responded by opening doors and bringing unexpected blessings into my life.

So, even if you find yourself in a place where you think you have nothing to invest in, remember that investing is not limited to financial resources alone. Your time, energy, talents, and kindness can also make a significant impact. Embrace the mindset of giving and receiving in a way that increases the joy of both yourself and others and allows the Universe to guide you toward opportunities for growth and abundance. Trust that the act of investing in yourself and others, no matter how small, can foster the unique offering you have to serve the world.

Exercise: Calling in Abundance with Acacia

Working with the acacia plant during the contemplative and detail-oriented Virgo season can be a profoundly transformative experience. Acacia, with its links to both spiritual and physical wealth through wellness, invites us to consider how we can invite more abundance into our world by focusing on how we can give instead of what we can get. Consider working with an acacia mala necklace. Count the beads of acacia wood while you recite affirmations about giving and receiving. Work with an acacia cutting board. Prepare food with awareness, paying attention to each careful slice, and giving thanks for the sustenance it provides to body and soul. During this time of introspection and Virgo's attention to detail, you can benefit from the acacia's insight into the nature of spiritual prosperity and the connection between the material and spiritual worlds.

Card Reflection: Abundance through Giving

Shuffle your deck and lay out five cards according to the spread below.

1. What is my current state of abundance?
2. Where can I be more generous in my life?
3. Where can I receive support in my life?
4. Where can I be grateful in my life?
5. What next step should I take?

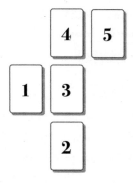

Affirmation

I give with an open heart, freely, graciously, with no expectation of return. I have exactly what I need. I create space for what I desire.

VIRGO II: SUFFICIENT FOR TODAY

Nine of Pentacles as Venus in Virgo

Living in financial abundance and flow means having exactly what you need in the present. You are not agonizing about past debts or future financial flows. When we learn how to use both the past and future to create the present, a portal to financial freedom opens.

MANIFESTING FINANCIAL PARTNERSHIPS

After a year or so on public assistance—while also working my way up from working part-time at the mall to my role as a teacher, and during a time of extreme burnout—I had to stop and consider what I was *really* designed to do. And I couldn't do it alone.

At the time, I had a partner who'd just started working. We were able to consolidate our expenses. We lived together, and we were well within our means to ensure that I had the time, space, resources, and energy to uncover the best use of my skills, experience, and desires. My partner was one of those people born knowing their purpose. But me? I was the type who needed to explore my options and take time to process the emotions that I kept choosing not to feel. I had to come back to my Self, heal my inner child, forgive those mentors, adults, and role models who I felt wronged by, and forgive all the past partners who had wronged me to find agreement with the Universe. Were it not for this energetic investment in the form of partnership, the financial flow I was to experience later would not have come into form. And even though I contributed less money to the partnership, I was fortunate to have a partner who understood the economic value in me taking on all the cleaning, cooking, and administrative responsibilities of the home.

Partnership can be the first step to healing burnout. Like the Hermit card, there are moments when working solo is necessary. But if we make it our sole method of operation, we miss the benefits of collaboration.

Exercise: Accounting and Consolidating Financial Resources

Consolidating expenses and resources can help heal burnout and help you live a more tranquil, conscious life within your means.

- **Identify Financial Stressors and Triggers:** Consider the factors that contribute to burnout in your life. Do you have high debt, no savings, financial uncertainty, or are you living paycheck to paycheck? Understanding these pressures will improve your management.

- **Identify Potential Financial Partners:** Consider individuals in your life who may be potential financial partners. A spouse, family, close friends, or trusted financial counselor could do it. Consider their financial strength, values, and readiness to share expenses and resources.

- **Identify How to Merge Resources:** Consider merging spending and resources with your financial partner to reap the rewards. How would this reduce financial stress and strengthen the foundation? Consider sharing bills, resources, and financial responsibilities. Make sure you have a written agreement in place that you can refer to in case a conflict arises. Have a plan for how to manage conflict, if it arises.

Financial stress affects your well-being, so embrace partnerships and live within your means to heal burnout and build financial security.

Affirmation

I trust that the Universe supports my desire for stress-free and prosperous financial partnerships. As I continue to cultivate positive beliefs and take inspired action, the perfect collaborators come into my life at the perfect time.

OPEN TO RECEIVE FINANCIAL ABUNDANCE WITH THE KNIGHT OF PENTACLES

Growing up in a single-income household with four children, I was familiar with a lack of material resources. In middle school, it became so obvious that I had only a few outfits on rotation that between that and my severe acne, I was a frequent target of bullies. At the age of 14, I started working at a fast-food restaurant 40 to 50 hours a week, just so I could have money to buy clothes and food I wanted to eat at school lunch. When I graduated college, I miscalculated the financial requirements for leading an independent life as a young adult. After relocating to a new city, I quickly exhausted my savings before securing employment. One day, I was struck by the reality that I had neither food nor the funds to buy any. Fortunately, I managed to obtain temporary government assistance from the social services office and accepted the first job I found—a part-time position as a retail associate at a local mall. The income I earned barely covered my expenses for food, bus fare, and a 10-dollar pair of shoes that I wore through the snowstorms of upstate New York. Because money was so tight, I had to learn very quickly how to create and adhere to an intentional spending plan, complete with a proper cash flow analysis, if I wanted to eat and have a roof over my head.

This experience heightened my awareness of my financial situation and the need for improved financial management. When I transitioned into a teaching career, I attended a presentation at a local church on Dave Ramsey's Financial Peace University. I learned to assign every dollar to a purpose, just as Marie Kondo would find a place for each item in our homes. This perspective helped me view my financial situation as a balance sheet, enabling me to assess my assets, liabilities, equity, and cash flow.

Utilizing a financial planning app for support, I gradually became proficient in managing my finances independently. I cultivated gratitude for what I had in the present moment, adopting the mindset that I always had everything I needed—no more and no less. This shift in thinking allowed me to tap into my intuition during challenging times, finding creative solutions and leveraging my financial resources effectively.

Tarot Meditation: Creating a Portal of Financial Flow

The Knight of Pentacles invites stability, responsibility, and practicality into our financial lives. As you visualize your desired financial future, you can picture yourself making deliberate choices that align with your financial goals. This includes embracing the wisdom to manage your *cash flow*—the equilibrium that exists in space-time between your assets and your liabilities.

Begin by finding a serene and comfortable place where you can unwind without distractions. Allow yourself a few moments to get settled and ready for your meditation. Close your eyes and take a deep breath, letting your body and mind relax. Picture yourself enveloped in a golden light that wraps you in tranquility and security.

In your mind's eye, conjure the image of the Knight of Pentacles tarot card. See the knight standing tall and confident, clutching a pentacle symbolizing wealth and abundance. As you connect with the energy of the Knight of Pentacles, imagine yourself stepping into a portal of financial flow. Visualize this portal as a golden and silver gateway filled with vibrant hues, diamonds, and shimmering light.

Feel an irresistible pull toward this portal, knowing it holds the key to forging a harmonious relationship with your finances. Trust that this portal will assist you in manifesting the abundance you seek. Take a moment to contemplate your current financial situation. Without passing judgment, observe any areas where you feel restricted in your finances. Consider how often you check your bank account, where you are circulating your money, and whether you have a spending plan.

Guided by the Knight of Pentacles, set your intention to create a portal of financial flow through financial planning, intentional spending, and getting support from professionals, like an accountant, where you need to. Picture yourself embracing the practice of planning your expenditure in advance, allocating your resources with purpose and clarity.

Visualize each decision you make concerning your finances becoming imbued with intention and awareness. See yourself making choices that align with your values and long-term goals, ensuring a steady and abundant flow of wealth into your life. Feel the energy of the portal supporting you as you cultivate discipline and responsibility in your financial habits. Sense the portal opening doors to new opportunities and income streams, attracting abundance from unexpected sources.

As you continue to meditate within the portal of financial flow, repeat affirmations that resonate with you. For example, "I am a wise steward of my financial resources," or "I attract abundance through intentional and mindful spending." Take a few moments to express gratitude for the financial flow that is already present in your life. Acknowledge any progress you have made on your financial journey, no matter how small.

When you're ready to conclude your meditation, take a deep breath and visualize yourself stepping out of the portal, carrying the energy of financial flow with you into your daily life. Open your eyes, feeling grounded and empowered. Carry the intention of budgeting and intentional spending with you throughout your day, knowing that you are creating a portal of financial flow that will usher abundance into your life.

Exercise: Create a Financial Tracker and Spending Plan

1. Gather financial information (bank statements, loan documents, etc.).

2. List your assets (cash, investments, property, etc.).

3. Calculate your liabilities (mortgages, loans, credit card debt, etc.).

4. Determine your net financial worth by subtracting liabilities from assets.

5. Analyze spending habits and categorize expenses.

6. Set realistic financial goals.

7. Create a monthly spending plan based on income, expenses, and savings.

8. Regularly monitor and adjust the spending plan to stay on track.

Card Reflection: Message from the Knight of Pentacles

Choose one tarot card. This is the message that the Knight of Pentacles has for you as you open the portal to more financial freedom, abundance, and flow.

Affirmation

I attract opportunities for growth and wealth through my practice of consciously allocating my resources to align with my financial goals.

VIRGO III: CONNECTING PAST WITH PRESENT WITH FUTURE

Ten of Pentacles as Mercury in Virgo

Consider your legacy as the narrative of your life, the story that you author with every choice, every action, and every inter-action. It is the enduring footprint that you etch on the canvas of time. It extends beyond the tangible confines of property or wealth. It also includes intangible yet profound facets of tra-ditions, accomplishments, abilities, and principles. The legacy you establish is your enduring message to eternity.

LEGACY THROUGH STEWARDSHIP

In our journey through life, we are entrusted with possessions and resources by the Universe. This divine trust calls us to be responsible stewards, taking care of and managing these resources wisely. However, the inefficient transfer of wealth across genera-tions and the lack of recycling assets back into the economic eco-system through new business creation or reinvestment to improve existing local communities have contributed to the many chal-lenges we face as a society.

To address this, we need to shift our perspective and embrace a new—yet old—approach: estate planning.

Estate planning is not just for the affluent. Estate planning begins with a simple action—*an inventory of what you have and how you are circulating it.* Unfortunately, the majority of individ-uals lack an estate plan for a variety of reasons. In my practice as an attorney, I see that the core challenge preventing many from estate planning is the absence of a concrete financial plan. When we operate without a strategic approach to our finances, we diminish our capacity to accumulate meaningful wealth. This, in turn, lessens the perceived need to strategize the redistribution of our assets to other organizations or succeeding generations, as would be facilitated by an estate plan. It's a gentle reminder of the importance of planning—not just for the present but for the future as well.

Estate planning is not just about finances, however. It considers both tangible property interests, like money and houses, as well as intangible interests, such as culture, spiritual values, and family or group rituals. It also addresses important matters such as healthcare directives, guardianship of minor children, pets, intellectual property, and the establishment of trusts for charitable giving or special needs individuals. It also provides an opportunity to minimize tax liability, ensure the smooth transfer of wealth between generations, and maintain privacy and confidentiality.

A lot of people don't like talking about death and taxes. But this is the reality in which we live. If you prefer a more capitalist-free approach to life—envisioning intergenerational collectives as microgovernments within the larger societal framework—estate planning is even more necessary. As our ancestors have learned and codified into numerous constitutions around the globe, there are to be clear distinctions about who owns what in order to minimize interpersonal conflict and avoid war between clashing cultures.

By adopting this approach, you ensure that future generations benefit from the lessons you have learned and the progress you made. At its core, this estate planning, reimagined, is about building a better future, today through interconnectedness and community. The smaller and more relational the community, the more people we need to acquire governance ability and the ability to lead micro-communities.

Exercise: What Kind of Ancestor Do You Want to Be?

Close your eyes and envision your future self. Imagine the life you've lived and the loved ones surrounding you. Now, consider what lessons you would like to leave for future generations, if any.

Grab a pen and paper. Write down your aspirations, dreams, and values. Think about who you trust to manage your assets and make decisions on your behalf. Reflect on healthcare directives, guardianship arrangements, and charitable giving. Embrace the emotions that arise, recognizing that discussing end-of-life matters is an act of love. By facing these topics head-on, you empower yourself and your loved ones to navigate the future with peace of mind.

Card Reflection: Message from the Hierophant to the Hermit about Estate Planning

The Hierophant is a significant card in the tarot deck that symbolizes tradition, wisdom, and guidance. It represents the spiritual leader, the one who imparts knowledge and teachings to others. In the context of the previous discussion on estate planning, the Hierophant reminds the Virgo Hermit of the importance of seeking guidance and wisdom when navigating the complexities of this process.

Just as the Hierophant serves as a guide in spiritual matters, estate planning requires thoughtful consideration and expert advice. It urges us to seek out professionals who can provide the necessary knowledge and expertise to help us make informed decisions about our assets, beneficiaries, and overall contribution to the legacy that is humanity. Furthermore, the Hierophant reminds us of the significance of tradition and the wisdom passed down through generations. We can draw upon their wisdom as we shape our estate plans, ensuring that our actions align with our values and contribute positively to the lives of those who come after us.

Place the Hermit card and the Hierophant card side by side. Tap into your intuition and request that Source provide you with a message or next step concerning the intergenerational transfer of resources.

Affirmation

I attract abundance and financial prosperity, using money to uplift my energetic frequency, transform my life, while reinvesting the surplus to transform my local community.

CULTIVATING EMPATHY FOR OUR ANCESTORS

Every choice we have made or will make gets passed to those who come after us. At birth, we all inherit privileges from our ancestors—some of us are raised in homes with great material, relational, intellectual, and spiritual wealth. Others are born with much less. These differences in wealth set the initial tone for the life we live. While some gaps can be bridged through hard work, divine connections can also play a role in how certain opportunities unfold. While it may seem unfair—and is, in some cases—that not everyone starts with the same social or economic advantages, the key lies in accepting our current reality, understanding our ancestors, learning from their wisdom, and improving on their failures.

The Iroquois of the Haudenosaunee understood the significance of passing down wisdom to future generations. With their "seventh generation thinking," they recognized that the actions and decisions made today could impact those living hundreds of years in the future. This long-term mindset urges us to adapt our thinking and consider the legacy we wish to leave behind. How do we want to be remembered by future generations who inherit our wealth?

The founders of the United States of America embodied a similar principle. Through their experiences with absolute rule and the failings of the Articles of Confederation, they created a collective agreement, called the U.S. Constitution, that found a balance between spiritual principles and practical realities. They aimed to create a framework that could withstand changing times while reflecting centuries old wisdom, back to ancient times. Although imperfect, the U.S. Constitutional system ultimately incentivizes self-governance and controlled evolution, by providing processes that allow for pushing back and ensuring a better future.

Our elders carry the wisdom of our ancestors and hold the promise of a brighter tomorrow. In a society focused on youthfulness and independence, we must not neglect the wisdom of our ancestors. By appreciating their institutions, values, and contributions, we can move forward together. Let us take the time to empathize with the worlds in which they lived.

Exercise: Making Peace with our Ancestors with Planetary Transits

Richard Tarnas's book, *Cosmos and Psyche: Intimations of a New World View*, explores the profound connections between astrology and historical events. Drawing on years of research and the insights of thinkers from Plato to Jung, Tarnas proposes that planetary transits hold significant correlations with epochal events such as the French Revolution. By studying these astrological transits, we can gain insight into past events and anticipate future developments.

With this knowledge, we can appreciate the impact of our ancestors' choices and ideologies, recognizing their role in shaping the world we inherit. By gaining a deeper understanding of historical events through the lens of astrology, we can uncover hidden patterns, motivations, and underlying forces that guide human behavior. This awareness allows us to navigate present challenges with wisdom and empathy, working toward a more harmonious and equitable society.

Card Reflection: Compassion for Ancestors

Shuffle your deck and lay out nine cards according to the spread below.

1. How have ancestral influences and historical events shaped your past?

2. What current cosmic energies are you feeling connected to and how are they impacting you?

3. If given the opportunity, what words or messages would you like to communicate to your ancestors?

4. Can you identify any barriers that might be hindering your empathy toward your ancestors?

5. What practices could you implement to cultivate a deeper understanding and empathy for your ancestors?

6. Is there any celestial wisdom or guidance that you feel drawn to receive?

7. How can you integrate these insights into your personal growth?

8. Are there any next steps you want to take?

9. Final advice from your spirit guides?

Affirmation

I acknowledge that my ancestors' actions were influenced by their own experiences, limitations, and societal norms, I seek to understand their perspectives and do my part to leave the world better today than it was yesterday.

THE DECANS OF LIBRA

Beauty
Truth
Love
Justice
Harmony
Peace
Balance

Imbalance
War
Dissonance
Injustice
Indifference
Falsehood
Beauty

LIBRA I: SEEING
YOURSELF IN THE OTHER

Two of Swords as Moon in Libra

Our beliefs allow us to construct meaning and order out of our lives. Our beliefs give a sense of purpose and inspire us to act. But when we are too certain of our beliefs, they may invite us to engage in intentional or unintentional harm as we seek safety in controlling others.

A BELIEF THAT'S WORTH HAVING IS WORTH QUESTIONING

In life, we often hold on to beliefs that shape our identity and guide our actions. These beliefs can come from various sources, such as personal experiences, cultural influences, or the wisdom of admired individuals. However, it is crucial to recognize the power of questioning our beliefs and remaining open to new perspectives.

When I stumbled upon an interview with Steve Jobs, his words resonated deeply with me. In a rare interview, he said, "I don't think anybody should be a lawyer, but going to law school can actually be useful because it teaches you how to think in a certain way." Until recently, I hadn't considered law school as an institution that shapes your thinking. I merely perceived it as a place that molds you into a lawyer. However, being a math teacher, I was able to make the following analogy: math class went beyond just right or wrong answers; it was about fostering critical thinking skills. Law school, then, was likely similar.

We can sometimes become so entrenched in our beliefs that we fear questioning them. We worry that by doing so, we might lose a part of ourselves or betray our roots. However, in law school we learn to embrace the practice of questioning, we open ourselves up to growth and expanded understanding.

The Socratic Method serves as a powerful tool for exploring various viewpoints on a single issue, enabling us to uncover and articulate the underlying and overt biases shaping our perspectives. This approach transforms the act of presenting differing views from a battle of victors and losers into a creative process. It's about offering as many perspectives as possible, selecting what we believe is the most compelling, all while acknowledging its inherent limitations. A tangible example of this in practice can be seen in a closely contested Supreme Court ruling, with a 5-4 vote and accompanying concurring and dissenting opinions.

Another way we learn how to become more mentally flexible, is by interpreting situations through different lenses such as text, history, tradition, precedent, structure, prudence, and morality with each interpretative lens having its own advantages and disadvantages.

Questioning beliefs does not mean discarding them entirely but rather enhancing our understanding and gaining deeper insights. By doing so, we cultivate a mindset that is open to growth and receptive to new information. We become more adaptable, compassionate, and capable of driving positive change.

So, let us consciously embark on a journey of self-inquiry, regularly examining our beliefs and why we hold them. By doing so, we honor our personal growth, contribute to collective well-being, and create a world where diverse perspectives are valued and celebrated.

Exercise: Trying on Different Beliefs with the Four Elements

On our healing journey, maintaining an open mind and a willingness to explore different beliefs is crucial. Instead of clinging to a single perspective, we can expand our horizons by embracing alternative viewpoints. One method to engage with this process is by employing the elements of the tarot to practice trying on different beliefs regarding a controversial topic.

By associating various beliefs with the elements present in the tarot—such as Earth (Pentacles), Water (Cups), Air (Swords), and Fire (Wands)—we can approach controversial topics from multiple angles. For instance, we can examine the practical, tangible aspects of an issue through the lens of Earth, considering the material and societal implications. Alternatively, we can delve into the emotional and intuitive aspects by analyzing the topic through the element of Water.

Furthermore, by exploring the intellectual and analytical dimensions using the element of Air, we can gain insights into the underlying principles and logical arguments related to the subject. Lastly, we can explore the passionate and dynamic aspects by examining the topic through the element of Fire, taking into account the energy, inspiration, and collective values involved.

By actively engaging in this exercise, we challenge our own assumptions and broaden our understanding of differing perspectives on the controversial topic at hand. This practice enhances our ability to empathize with others, fostering a more compassionate and inclusive worldview. Remember, the goal is not necessarily to adopt a specific belief, but rather to cultivate empathy and expand our capacity for understanding.

Card Reflection: Changing Lenses

This tarot card spread is designed to help you explore different elemental energies and perspectives on a controversial topic. Shuffle your tarot deck and choose cards one by one, until you have one of each element—earth, water, air, and fire. If you draw the same element multiple times, decide if you want to keep or discard that card.

For each element, consider:

1.   **Earth (Pentacles)** — This card represents the practical, tangible aspects of the topic. What are the material implications? How does society or the physical world come into play?

2.   **Water (Cups)** — This card delves into the emotional and intuitive aspects. How do people's feelings and emotions influence their beliefs on this topic? What are the underlying motivations?

3. **Air (Swords)** — This card explores the intellectual and analytical dimensions. What are the logical arguments and principles at play? How do different ideas clash or align?

4. **Fire (Wands)** — This card examines the passionate and dynamic aspects. What are the energy, inspiration, and collective values involved? How do differing perspectives fuel the debate?

5. **Integration** — This card represents the synthesis of the four elemental energies. What insights have you gained from exploring these perspectives? What new understanding or empathy has emerged?

As you interpret each card, reflect on how it relates to the controversial topic at hand and how it challenges or expands your own beliefs.

Affirmation

I release the need to cling to a single perspective. I embrace the richness of alternative viewpoints and a lifestyle that promotes mental flexibility.

DECONSTRUCTING BELIEFS WITH THE ASTEROID GODDESSES

As an air sign ruled by Venus, Libra brings its unique energy to the deconstruction of limiting beliefs. Libra is known for its desire for fairness, harmony, and balance, making it the perfect lens to examine our beliefs. By harnessing Libra's energy, we can approach our self-reflection with diplomacy, grace, and a commitment to creating equilibrium in our thoughts and actions.

In our journey of personal growth and self-discovery, we have the power to transform our lives by recognizing and questioning the beliefs we hold. By embarking on the process of deconstructing our beliefs, we can let go of those that no longer serve us and create new paradigms better suited for our present reality.

The journey of deconstructing beliefs is not a one-time event; rather, it is a constant cycle of unraveling, releasing, and rebuilding. We encounter deconstruction when our old binaries are challenged with information that introduces greater ambiguity into our lives. It is in these moments that we can explore the depths of our beliefs and reshape our understanding of the world.

During the deconstruction process, we may encounter resistance in the form of cognitive dissonance. This occurs when our set of ideas, attitudes, beliefs, or opinions clashes with those of others, creating contradictions. These contradictions shake our sense of safety and predictability, demanding that we invest more energy into understanding the nuances of the situation.

Living in a world driven by competition for scarce resources, it may seem like a disadvantage to dedicate attention and energy to understanding nuance rather than seeing things in black and white. However, in a world where collaboration is valued over competition, the ability to navigate through dissonance and arrive at a state of interdependence becomes a profound advantage. This not only benefits the individual but also contributes to the well-being of the collective.

In a world where change is constant, the ability to question and deconstruct our beliefs becomes an invaluable tool for personal evolution. By embracing the inherent ambiguity of life, we expand our perspectives, deepen our understanding, and cultivate resilience in the face of uncertainty.

Exercise: Power Rebalancing with the Asteroid Goddesses

This exercise connects the four great Asteroid Goddesses—Ceres, Pallas Athene, Vesta, and Juno—to the tarot card representing Libra, Temperance. You will gain insights and heal by deconstructing beliefs holding power over your life.

- **Ceres—Explore Self-Care.** Reflect on your self-care beliefs. Note any opinions or beliefs. Question these beliefs: Are they helping you? Are these cultural expectations or true understanding? Accept the wisdom of Ceres, the goddess of nurture and motherhood, and let go of any limiting ideas that prevent you from prioritizing self-care. Affirm your worthiness of love and care and commit to self-care for healing and growth.

- **Pallas Athena—Explore Intellectual Freedom.** Explore your intellectual beliefs, including any self-imposed or societally enforced constraints. Challenge these ideas by connecting with Pallas Athena, the goddess of wisdom and strategy. Free yourself from outdated thinking and embrace your unique intellectual ability. Celebrate your freedom to speak and accept different viewpoints. Free yourself from mental constraints and explore new learning chances.

- **Vesta—Explore Authenticity.** Consider your passion and convictions. Does fear or society prevent you from expressing your passions and living authentically? Inspire your fire with Vesta, the goddess of the hearth and sacred flame. Let go of limiting beliefs and follow your passions. Declare your authenticity and share your talents. Enjoy the freedom of being yourself.

- **Juno—Explore Inequality.** Examine your commitment and relationship beliefs. Are there any beliefs that limit your freedom or perpetuate inequality? Reconsider these views with Juno, the goddess of loyalty and partnership. Declare your commitment to equal and respectful relationships. Let rid of assumptions that limit your relationship freedom and embrace connections that honor and support your uniqueness.

To work more with the Asteroid Goddesses, I suggest *Asteroid Goddesses: The Mythology, Psychology, and Astrology of the Re-emerging Feminine* by Demetra George and Douglas Bloch.

Card Reflection: Asteroid Healing

Shuffle your deck and lay out seven cards according to the spread below.

1. What is your belief about self-care and how does it nurture you?

2. Can you identify any subconscious limitations that might be hindering your intellectual freedom and self-expression?

3. Are there any beliefs rooted in past trauma that are preventing you from expressing your true passion and authenticity?

4. Can you pinpoint and break down any beliefs that may be limiting the freedom within your relationships and fostering inequality?

5. Do you experience any resistance or emotions when you attempt to challenge your limiting beliefs?

6. Can you imagine the positive transformations and new opportunities that could arise from letting go of these beliefs?

7. What next step should you take?

Affirmation

I embrace ambiguity and explore the depths of my beliefs to reshape my understanding of the world.

QUESTIONING "SPIRITUAL, BUT NOT RELIGIOUS"

In his book, *Religious but Not Religious*, Jason E. Smith delves into Carl Jung's idea that the religious sense is intrinsic to our psyche. According to Jung, our lack of this sense has adverse effects.

Symbolic forms of religion add meaning and purpose to our lives. Therefore, we cannot ignore the decline of traditional religious observance, which is becoming more prevalent. Losing the accumulated spiritual wisdom of ancient religions would be detrimental to the human soul.

As humans, we yearn for spiritual experiences. While being "spiritual but not religious" is one response, it often falls short. It can easily become a shallow form of self-guided spirituality that lacks true growth and transformation, which are the aims of religious traditions.

Smith argues that we should adopt a "religious but not religious" approach. This means recognizing the importance of both individual spiritual adventures and collective religious traditions. Religion, in this view, becomes a participation in the symbolic life rather than a mere set of beliefs. By reconnecting with our sensitivity to symbolic experiences and understanding religion symbolically, we open ourselves to profound encounters with life and the human condition. These encounters can then be tested, experienced, and transformed.

Exercise: Cultivating a Symbolic Understanding of Religion

Lemons, with their vibrant yellow hue and tangy zest, hold a fascinating metaphorical power that extends beyond their culinary and medicinal uses. Lemons serve as potent symbols of purification and cleansing, inviting us to examine our own beliefs and let go of what no longer serves us. Just as the sourness of a lemon can initially cause discomfort, the process of challenging our beliefs can be uncomfortable. However, it is through this process that we gain clarity and transform ourselves, just as the sour lemon transforms into a refreshing lemonade. So, let us embrace the lessons of the lemon, allowing it to inspire us to deconstruct our beliefs, challenge the status quo, and embark on a journey of personal and spiritual growth.

To work with lemon as plant medicine during Libra season:

1. **Lemon Electrolyte Water:** Start your day by drinking a glass of lemon water. Squeeze the juice of half a lemon into a glass of water and enjoy it upon waking. This refreshing drink acts as a balancing and cleansing elixir, providing hydration and electrolytes to kickstart your day.

2. **Lemon Detox Diet:** Consider incorporating the lemon water diet into your routine. This involves drinking lemon water throughout the day, either as a detox or weight loss regimen. Remember to consult a healthcare professional before starting any restrictive diet.

3. **Cleansing Rituals:** Use lemons in purification and cleansing rituals to release negativity and stagnant energy. Burn lemon-infused incense or diffuse lemon essential oil during meditation to create an atmosphere of rejuvenation and clarity. Visualize the purifying properties of lemons, allowing them to cleanse your mind and soul, and create space for personal transformation during Libra season.

Remember, working with lemon as plant medicine is not a substitute for professional medical advice. It is always recommended to consult a healthcare professional before making any significant changes to your diet or wellness routine.

Card Reflection: Examining Your Spiritual Beliefs

Use this spread to delve into your spiritual and religious journey, exploring the different aspects of your beliefs and practices. Reflect on these questions and draw seven cards to gain insights and guidance.

1. What aspects of your life hold a deep sense of meaning and connection to the divine?

2. What rituals, traditions, or beliefs do you follow as part of a specific religious path or community?

3. Where do your spiritual beliefs align with your religious traditions?

4. Where do you not resonate strongly with either spirituality or religious practices?

5. Why?

6. Strengths and positive qualities of your spiritual and religious beliefs?

7. One area to focus your attention and efforts for personal growth?

8. Next step or direction on your spiritual and religious path?

Affirmation

I connect with my sensitivity to symbolic experiences, opening myself to profound encounters that expand my understanding of life and the human condition.

LIBRA II: THE POWER
OF AGREEMENT

Three of Swords as Saturn in Libra

Getting into energetic agreement with the collective requires that we invest some of our self-interest for the benefit of the collective interest. The best negotiations end when all sides receive something, but all sides lose something too.

FINDING AGREEMENT

In spiritual circles, the concept of alignment often comes up in our quest for harmony. We seek alignment with the Universe, ourselves, and others. However, the idea of alignment can be misleading. It suggests that we should be the same, perfectly aligned.

A more fitting word to describe what we truly seek is agreement. Finding agreement with ourselves, others, and the Universe is essential. While there may be areas where we lack alignment, if we unite toward a common goal, we invest in bringing collective interests into form. This collective effort propels us forward on the evolutionary path we choose.

When striving for agreement, it can be disheartening to let go of something. Our nervous system craves safety, acceptance, and control. Yet, by allowing ourselves time to find common ground, we can maintain a sense of security. Gradually, we can progress in sync with the collective evolutionary forces.

Similarly, it can be disappointing when we no longer find agreement with people who were once aligned with us. We understand their perspective, the pros and cons, but the gap between us becomes too wide. And that's okay. Trust in the Universal force. It will guide your relationships to an outcome that benefits all of humanity. Focus on what you can control and surround yourself with those who are within your zone of agreement.

In the pursuit of agreement, it's helpful to remember the Pareto principle, also known as the 80-20 rule. We find agreement when we share about 80 percent alignment with someone else's ideas. The remaining 20 percent, although uncomfortable, invites us to evolve in understanding, compassion, and action for the greater good.

Sometimes, however, agreement is simply not possible, and we must consider severing ties. The founders of the United States of America confronted this reality on July 4, 1776, during Saturn's presence in Libra. The Declaration of Independence stands as a poetic political document, where 56 signers from diverse backgrounds came together around a common grievance. They exhausted all other avenues for resolution and appealed to the "Supreme Judge of the world" under the shelter of "divine Providence." They recognized that drastic measures, like war or separation, should not be taken lightly, but are justified when a long history of abuses and usurpations threaten the very essence of Nature itself. They understood that sometimes separation can lead to a renewed sense of agreement. Time apart allows each party to rediscover themselves as individuals before reuniting in a new form, whether it be a new organization, different local governments, or a blended family.

In our journey toward agreement, let us remain open to the possibilities of unity, evolution, and separation when necessary. Trust in the process, embrace growth, and remember that the pursuit of collective harmony is a path worth pursuing.

Exercise: Exploring Alignment Versus Agreement

In this exercise, take time for reflective writing to delve into your personal definition of alignment and agreement. Consider how these concepts have influenced your relationships and decision-making processes. Next, evaluate your current relationships to determine if there is a healthy balance between seeking agreement and maintaining your individual values and boundaries. Identify areas in your life where clearer boundaries may be necessary to establish a sense of agreement within yourself and with others. Practice effective communication techniques that foster understanding and seek agreement while respecting different perspectives. Lastly, apply the Pareto principle to analyze your commitments and relationships, identifying the vital few (20 percent) that bring the most fulfillment. Focus your energy on nurturing those connections to further connect your life with what truly matters.

Card Reflection: Agreeing to Agree

Shuffle your deck and lay out seven cards according to the spread below.

1. What is the issue?
2. Where are places for agreement?
3. Where are areas for disagreement?
4. Where are places for movement?
5. Where are places you need to stay in place?
6. Where can you apply the 80-20 principle?
7. What next steps should you take?

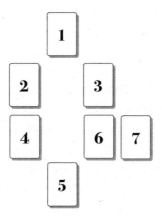

Affirmation

I focus on what I can control and surround myself with individuals who are within my zone of agreement.

MUTUALLY BENEFICIAL AGREEMENTS WITH JUSTICE AND THE EMPRESS

In this intricate and interconnected world, Justice and the Empress serve as guiding forces to remind us of the importance of embodying the principles of mutual benefit and consideration for our individual and collective well-being. Justice acts as a beacon of fairness, balance, and impartiality, urging us to base our decisions on equitable principles while taking into account the needs and perspectives of all involved. By seeking harmony and resolution through thoughtful deliberation and objective judgment, we pave the way for positive outcomes. On the other hand, the Empress embodies abundance, nurturing, and creativity, highlighting the strength found in collaboration and mutual support. When we embrace the unique strengths and contributions of others, we create fertile ground for growth and prosperity.

In his influential book, *The 7 Habits of Highly Effective People*, Stephen Covey teaches us how to turn competition into collaboration. Instead of perceiving situations as win-lose scenarios, he encourages us to find solutions that benefit everyone involved. This shift in perspective opens up a realm of abundance and possibilities, where cooperation becomes a catalyst for success.

We are interdependent beings and the pursuit of mutual benefit encourages us to support one another. It goes beyond self-interest at the expense of others. By aligning our goals and actions with the betterment of all, we foster unity and create outcomes that empower everyone involved.

This approach of mutual benefit becomes particularly vital when addressing societal challenges such as inequality, environmental degradation, and political polarization. By embracing a win-win mindset, we rise above rigid ideologies and seek common ground. We focus on shared problems and work collaboratively toward solutions that bridge divides and foster inclusivity. The result is a more equitable and harmonious world, where understanding and cooperation prevail.

However, embodying a win-win mindset requires emotional intelligence and maturity. It calls for the ability to express our thoughts and convictions while genuinely considering the perspectives and feelings of others. This level of maturity allows us to engage in constructive dialogue, cultivate empathy, and navigate disagreements with grace and respect. By continuously practicing and nurturing this mindset, we can create a world where mutual benefit and consideration are the guiding principles for our personal and collective growth.

Exercise: Drafting a Mutually Beneficial Agreement

Reflect on an agreement or goal you would like to achieve that involves mutual benefit and collaboration. It could be a personal or professional endeavor.

Consider how each planetary archetype can be incorporated into your written agreement:

Moon: Consider the intention, energy, and objective behind proposing this agreement.

Sun: Identify the involved parties and the nature of the agreement.

Saturn: Set the scope and limits of the agreement.

Jupiter: Think about how to accommodate future revisions to the terms of the agreement.

Mars: Specify the consequences if someone fails to adhere to the agreement.

Venus: Establish guidelines for future negotiations.

Mercury: Detail the modes and frequency of communication.

Write down your win-win agreement, incorporating the elements mentioned above and ensuring clarity, fairness, and balance between all parties involved.

Review and revise the agreement as needed, seeking input and feedback from the other party or legal professional, if applicable.

Sign and date the agreement, symbolizing your commitment to fostering a win-win spirit and mutual benefit in your interactions.

Remember, the key is to create an agreement that promotes collaboration, fairness, and positive outcomes for all involved. By consciously considering the planetary archetypes, you can infuse your agreement with intention and align it with principles that transcend individual interests, fostering a true win-win spirit.

Card Reflection: Brainstorming a Mutually Beneficial Agreement

Shuffle your deck and lay out ten cards according to the spread below.

1. **Scenario.** What are the background facts relevant to the negotiation?

2. **Issues.** What are your issues in relation to the scenario?

3. **Your Interests.** Why is the negotiation important to you?

4. **Their Interests.** Why is the negotiation important to them?

5. **Your Wants.** What is your best-case scenario?

6. **Their Wants.** What is their best-case scenario?

7. **Win-Win.** Where will you likely reach a middle ground?

8. **Alternative One.** Other potential outcome you would accept?

9. **Alternative Two.** Other potential outcome you would accept?

10. Next steps or preparation?

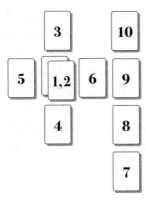

Affirmation

I create opportunities for mutual benefit and abundance, knowing that there is enough for everyone to thrive and succeed.

THE POWER OF NEGOTIATION WITH
THE QUEEN OF SWORDS

Negotiation is an essential skill that empowers us to navigate life's challenges and build harmonious relationships. However, many lack the knowledge and techniques to negotiate effectively. It's time to unlock the power of principled negotiation and achieve win-win outcomes that benefit both ourselves and others. By embracing this transformative approach, we can create a life filled with success, collaboration, and personal growth.

Principled negotiation, as taught by experts at the Harvard Negotiation Project, is the key to unlocking mutually beneficial agreements. It involves seeking common ground and resolving conflicts based on fair standards collectively agreed upon. This approach focuses on the merits of the issue at hand while maintaining respect and empathy for all parties involved. Through principled negotiation, we can harmoniously blend assertiveness and understanding, leading to outcomes where both people give and receive.

Negotiation is both an art and a science, requiring a delicate balance of hard and soft skills. Hard skills involve strategic planning, meticulous research, and a deep understanding of the facts and figures involved. On the other hand, soft skills encompass active listening, empathy, effective communication, and emotional intelligence. By mastering these skills, we can navigate complex negotiations with grace and confidence, ensuring success every step of the way.

Embracing principled negotiation as a way of life yields tremendous benefits. By prioritizing mutual gains and fairness, we not only achieve our individual goals but also foster stronger relationships built on trust, respect, and shared objectives. This approach encourages collaboration, sparks innovative problem-solving, and lays the foundation for long-lasting, sustainable partnerships. By temporarily setting aside our own interests, we open the door to endless possibilities for collaboration and collective prosperity.

Tarot Meditation: Preparing for Negotiation with the Queen of Swords

Close your eyes and take a deep breath. As you begin this tarot meditation, envision the image of the Queen of Swords. See her seated on a majestic throne, her back straight and her posture poised with grace. She wears a regal gown adorned with symbols of wisdom and insight. Her piercing gaze reveals a mind sharp and clear, reflecting her unwavering objectivity.

Take a moment to imagine the surroundings of the Queen of Swords. Picture a serene and tranquil environment, where the air is filled with a sense of calmness and clarity. This peaceful ambiance serves as a reminder to cultivate a similar state of mind as you prepare for negotiation.

Now, let us use the symbolism of the Queen of Swords as an analogy for the negotiation process. Just as the Queen embodies qualities of objectivity, clarity, and foresight, so too should we embody these qualities during our negotiations. Visualize yourself stepping into the role of the Queen of Swords, radiating confidence and wisdom.

As you continue with this meditation, consider the steps that can be taken during the negotiation process. See yourself gathering information, thoroughly researching the subject matter, and understanding all perspectives involved. Allow yourself to recognize both your strengths and weaknesses, acknowledging areas where further preparation may be required.

Now, visualize setting realistic goals for the negotiation. Envision yourself confidently articulating your desires and needs, while remaining open to finding common ground. Picture yourself engaging in constructive dialogue, maintaining your composure, and expressing your thoughts with eloquence and assertiveness.

As this tarot meditation comes to a close, visualize a successful outcome, where you achieve your desired goals while preserving harmony and goodwill. See yourself building strong and mutually beneficial relationships through this process.

Inhale deeply and exhale slowly, releasing any tension or doubt. Carry the energy of the Queen of Swords within you as you embark on your negotiation journey. Remember her qualities of objectivity, clarity, and foresight, allowing them to guide you toward a successful resolution.

When you are ready, gently open your eyes, feeling refreshed, confident, and prepared for the negotiation that lies ahead.

Affirmation

I approach negotiations with confidence and grace, knowing that I have the wisdom to navigate any challenges that arise.

LIBRA III: RISE UP SO YOU CAN RISE OUT

Four of Swords as Jupiter in Libra

Spiritual bypassing, which is neither inherently positive nor negative, involves using religious and spiritual practices to distance ourselves from our experiences. In our diverse and often conflict-ridden world, spiritual tools can provide us with a sanctuary, aiding in processing and resetting our perspectives. However, remaining in a state of spiritual bypass can inadvertently harm others if we neglect to employ our skills, gifts, and capabilities to support and contribute to the wider community. We are not in a position to dictate when others should take action or remain passive; such decisions are personal and should be made in consultation with the Universe. Our responsibility lies in syncing with our own rhythms and patterns, operating in a manner that respects the here and now, and allowing the Universe to be the ultimate decider.

FINDING SPIRITUAL TEMPERANCE

In your healing journey, you may often find yourself confronting intimidating obstacles and unresolved emotions that can seem overwhelming. Dissociation becomes a survival strategy, letting you temporarily retreat from the pain. It's a way to find sanctuary and shield your vulnerable heart. But authentic healing transcends dissociation.

To set foot on a healing path, you need to engage with rituals and archetypes that navigate you through the peaks and valleys. These age-old symbols and practices turn into guiding lights, steering you toward internal balance. They equip you with a structure to forge a life on your own terms, one deeply anchored in self-care and self-exploration.

During shared crises, it's common for individuals to resort to blaming and shaming as a means to regain control. However, healing teaches you that genuine power resides not in blame, but in comprehension and empathy. Instead of perpetuating the shame cycle, you have the option to embrace interdependence and accept the complexities of the world surrounding you.

Rather than strictly pursuing independence, consider aiming for interdependence—a state of interconnectedness where you recognize the impact of your actions on others and the environment. In a state of interdependence, an energy of acceptance is available. Acceptance allows us to release that which is out of our control. In this posture of acceptance, you channel your energy toward aspects that are truly transformable when you take action on them.

Healing isn't an endpoint, nor is it simply a path to follow. It is a perpetual cycle of energy transformation and transmutation, transitioning from one energetic form to another through the efficient utilization and recycling of resources. This process occurs at a pace that is not only suitable for you as an individual, but also for the collective. We evolve individually, then collectively.

Exercise: Pause

Take a moment to reflect on the themes of healing and interdependence explored in the previous passage. Find a quiet space where you can sit comfortably and close your eyes. Take a few deep breaths, allowing yourself to relax and let go of any tension. Picture yourself surrounded by a soft, golden light that represents healing energy. As you visualize this light, imagine it connecting you to all living beings, forming an ebbing and flowing web of interdependence. Feel the gentle support and connection flowing through this web. Allow yourself to absorb the wisdom of accepting what is beyond your control and focusing on what you can change. Embrace the seasons of rest and activity, acknowledging their importance in your healing journey. When you feel ready, slowly open your eyes, carrying this sense of interconnectedness with you throughout your day. Remember, we are all in this together, and by nurturing ourselves, we heal the world by healing ourselves.

Card Reflection: Navigating Spiritual Highs and Lows with Temperance

The Temperance card holds profound symbolism and offers guidance as you delve into the concept of spiritual bypassing.

1. **Identify the bypassing.** Where are you avoiding the facing of challenging emotions or situations by remaining in the comfort of spiritual practices or beliefs? Where are you passive? Where are you active?

2. **Identify your equilibrium.** Where is your harmonious middle ground between spirituality and facing the realities of life? How do you navigate the delicate dance between the spiritual and the mundane?

3. **Consider blending.** How may you integrate your spiritual practices with your emotional experiences? How can you use spirituality as a tool for healing and growth while also honoring the authenticity of your emotions? Explore ways to blend these aspects when called to blend?

4. **Resting in harmony.** Is this the harmony I strive for? Why or why not? Am I moving toward transformation and contribution to the community? Or do I continually rest in comfort?

Temperance serves as a reminder to find a place of moderation and integration in our spiritual paths. It encourages us to blend our spiritual practices with our emotional experiences, fostering inner harmony and growth. By embracing both the spiritual and the mundane, we can transcend the limitations of spiritual bypassing and embark on a more authentic and transformative journey.

Affirmation

I nurture a harmonious relationship between the spiritual and the mundane, finding beauty and wisdom in both realms.

WE ALL RISE AND FALL TOGETHER
WITH THE LUNAR NODES

Rising together is a potent theme embedded in our collective journey of growth and transformation. It underscores the idea that our individual healing and collective healing are intrinsically intertwined. This theme finds also deep resonance in the realms of psychology and astrology, particularly in the context of attachment theory vis-à-vis the lunar nodes.

Attachment theory proposed that humans have an inherent need to form strong bonds with others. These connections serve as a social safety net, distributing the impact of trauma across a group rather than isolating it to one individual. This mechanism, embedded within our brains, is designed to ensure our safety by fostering closeness with those we care about. However, when this safety net is missing, especially during childhood, we may resort to unhealthy coping strategies, such as becoming overly attached and losing our individuality within relationships.

The lunar nodes in astrology offer a spiritual perspective on this dynamic. They symbolize our past experiences and future potential, emphasizing the importance of balance and harmony as integral parts of our soul's journey. The alignment of these nodes with Jupiter in Libra and the Four of Swords tarot card paints a rich tapestry of interconnected energies.

Jupiter in Libra signifies growth and abundance in interpersonal relationships, encouraging us to seek harmony, balance, and diplomacy in our interactions. This celestial configuration fosters open communication and cooperation, promoting fairness and mutual understanding.

The Four of Swords, on the other hand, represents a period of rest and introspection. It urges us to step back from the hustle and bustle of life, creating space for rejuvenation and self-care. This state of tranquility allows us to approach our relationships from a place of peace and clarity.

In combination with the lunar nodes, these astrological influences underscore the significance of balanced communication, self-reflection, and honoring the karmic lessons inherent in our relationships. They encourage us to embrace fairness, inner peace, and alignment with our higher purpose, leading to deeper connections with others and personal growth.

Research has shown that the moon has a profound effect on the human body, influencing our sleep patterns, hormonal balance, and emotional well-being. The moon impacts our energy levels, mood, and behavior, just as it influences the ebb and flow of the tides. As we align ourselves with these cosmic rhythms, we can harness the moon's energy through knowledge of its nodal placement in our natal charts to enhance our healing process and foster harmonious relationships.

Exercise: Lunar Influences on Your Relationships

Step 1: Find your lunar nodes (North Node ☊ and South Node ☋) on your astrological natal chart. Many online resources can generate this using your birth details.

Step 2: Understand your lunar nodes. Relationships equilibrate between the North and South Nodes. While it may be time to move toward the North and away from the South node, the opposite could also apply—or even the integration of the nodes—depending on the situation. Reflect on these traits and how nodal equilibrium is manifesting in your life.

Step 3: Evaluate your relationships. Are there recurring patterns (South Node) or growth challenges (North Node)? Write about your findings.

Step 4: Based on your reflections, set intentions for your relationships. What patterns do you want to change? What new relationship behaviors do you want to develop?

Exercise: Reflecting on Your Attachments

What relationship you should consider?

Where you are anxious?

Where you are avoidant?

Where you are both anxious and avoidant?

How can you move toward secure attachment within this relationship?

What relationships should you invest more time in?

What relationships should you invest less time in?

Affirmation

I am committed to cultivating harmonious connections and honoring karmic lessons within my relationships.

THE DECANS OF SCORPIO

In the depths
Of our darkness
There's nothing
To find
But
Light

SCORPIO I: RITUALIZING LOSS

Five of Cups as Mars in Scorpio

We return from that which we were made. Energy is neither created nor destroyed. It merely transitions from one form to the next.

RITUAL AS A FORM OF SYMBOL

Rituals are integral to our existence. They bring order to the chaos of our lives, especially during periods of significant change, transition, and loss. They serve as symbolic bridges, helping us connect with others, the broader Universe, and those who have journeyed before us. Their potency lies not just in their symbolic value, but also in their ability to provide comfort by releasing endorphins that help ease anxiety and instill a sense of calm and tranquility.

Reflecting on my own life, I recall the weekly ritual of visiting the cemetery after church services during my childhood. This simple act brought me face to face with the cyclical nature of existence and our shared mortality. It also served as a tangible connection to my ancestors, reminding me that we are all part of a larger narrative. When my grandmother unexpectedly passed during the pandemic, I learned how to ritualize loss in a different way. Every year on her birthday I would send her flowers—and still do the same, even though the flowers are now placed by a grave. My grandmother lived in northern France during World War II, married an American soldier, and found her healing at America's shores. I felt like it was up to me to complete her cycle and place French lavender at her gravesite. To bring her finally back to her home, to the family in France that she lost through sickness and war.

My grandmother made her transition in the early morning with the one person at her side that I know she likely wanted to be there. She passed into the next world with no debts, no assets, no conflict. Just a few signatures and a moment of reflection and prayer. The only thing I have from my grandmother is a cross she gave to me on my seventh birthday—a cross that she was given by her parents at her first communion. It's the only thing I've kept from my childhood and is a reminder of her present energy that I hope to pass on when the time is right.

Life is a continuous flow of transformations, and the ability to see the eternal in the temporal is one way we can hold space for all the feelings that come up with loss.

Exercise: A Lesson from Water About Navigating Loss

Water moving with a current can be a powerful metaphor for understanding the process of navigating loss and transitions in our lives. In its simplest definition, a current refers to the continuous flow of water in a particular direction. It is often influenced by external forces such as tides, winds, or the shape of the land.

When we apply this concept to our own experiences of loss and transitions, we can see that these moments also involve a continuous movement forward, much like a current. Just as water is shaped and guided by external factors, we too are shaped by the circumstances and events that surround us during these times.

For this exercise, imagine standing at the edge of a river, watching the water flow with purpose and determination. Observe the water. See how it moves, it encounters various obstacles—rocks, branches, or changes in the riverbed. Consider how water, instead of resisting or getting stuck, adapts and finds its way around these challenges. It continues its journey, gradually wearing away at barriers and carving new paths.

Similarly, when we face loss or transition, we are confronted with obstacles and changes that can feel overwhelming and disorienting. Like water, however, we have the capacity to adapt and find new ways forward. We can learn to navigate through grief, uncertainty, and the unfamiliar, gradually finding our unique path through the currents of life.

It's important to note that water currents are not always smooth or linear. There may be times when it rushes with great force, crashing against rocks and creating turbulence. Similarly, our own journey through loss and transitions can be tumultuous, filled with emotions and uncertainties. But just as the water eventually calms and continues its steady flow, we too can find moments of peace and clarity amidst the chaos.

By embracing the fluidity of our experiences and accepting the natural currents that guide us, we can learn to process loss and transitions with greater resilience and grace. Like water, we can find strength in our ability to adapt, persist, and carve a new path forward. And as we navigate these currents, we may discover unexpected beauty, growth, and a deeper understanding of ourselves.

In the end, the metaphor of water moving with a current reminds us that we are not alone in our experiences of loss and transitions. We are part of a greater flow, interconnected with others who are also navigating their own journeys. By recognizing this interconnectedness and finding solace in the rhythm of life's currents, we can find comfort and strength as we move forward, embracing the ever-changing nature of our existence.

Affirmation

I am deserving of love, compassion, and self-care during this time of grief, allowing myself to prioritize my well-being and nurture my emotional needs.

REMEMBERING ALL SOULS

All Souls' Day, observed on November 2nd each year, is a significant day in many cultures and religious traditions around the world. It is a time when people come together to honor and remember their loved ones who have transitioned into another realm. On this day, prayers, rituals, and remembrance ceremonies take place to honor the souls of those who have passed away. It is believed that on All Souls' Day, the souls of the deceased are given an opportunity for comfort, forgiveness, and spiritual renewal. Families visit cemeteries to clean and decorate the graves of their loved ones, lighting candles and placing flowers as symbols of remembrance and love. All Souls' Day serves as a reminder of the interconnectedness between those on Earth, and those who have transitioned. Not only does this day offer solace, but it shifts your mind from one of linear timelines and consumption, to one that is focused on cycles, transitions, and devotion without expectation.

Exercise: Using the Onion to Connect with Your Ancestors

Onions, with their many layers, offer us a glimpse into the rich tapestry of cultural practices and ancestral wisdom. In the vibrant Mexican culture, onions take center stage during Día de los Muertos, where dishes prepared for ancestors often feature this versatile vegetable. This culinary tradition not only showcases the deep-rooted connection between onions and ancestral reverence but also reminds us of the layers of experience that shape our lives. Just as onions have hidden layers, so do our emotions and experiences. When we shed tears while chopping onions, we realize that sometimes we cry without understanding why, mirroring the complex layers of our own existence.

Close your eyes and imagine an onion plant in a serene garden. As you observe its layers, reflect on the various aspects of your being. Peel away the layers, releasing negativity and discovering your true essence. Embrace the core's energy and wisdom. Open your eyes, carrying the lessons of growth and inner strength with you.

Card Reflection: Message from the Ancestors

To create a sacred space, find a quiet place and light a candle or incense to honor your ancestors. Close your eyes and visualize a serene path leading to a beautiful garden with a meeting place. Call upon your ancestors, be open to their messages, and engage in conversation. Express gratitude and return to the present moment. Journal for deeper understanding. Revisit this exercise to reconnect with your ancestral lineage and tap into their wisdom and love.

Shuffle your deck and lay out seven cards side by side.

1. **Foundation:** Represents the essence of ancestral connection.

2. **Ancestor's Message:** Offers direct guidance from an ancestor.

3. **Ancestral Guidance:** Provides suggestions to strengthen the bond.

4. **Lessons Learned:** Reveals inherited qualities or teachings.

5. **Ancestral Healing:** Identifies unresolved ancestral wounds.

6. **Ancestral Blessings:** Highlights ancestral support and gifts.

7. **Integration:** Guides incorporating wisdom into daily life.

   Reflect on each card, record insights, and revisit as needed.

Affirmation

I feel gratitude as I connect with and remember my loved ones who have transitioned.

SCORPIO II: HOLDING SPACE FOR ALL EMOTIONS

Six of Cups as Sun in Scorpio

We cry not because of who we are becoming, but because we mourn the loss of who we once were. We grieve the past because it is there where we loved. Grief is love so abundant that it emanates in our very being. It is the holiness of not becoming, but of becoming undone.

NAMING EMOTIONS

Emotions possess a mighty and profound force, capable of propelling us to soaring heights or plunging us into the depths of despair. They are the vibrant colors that paint the canvas of our lives, infusing each moment with passion and intensity. It is through the raw power of emotions that we find the ability to shape and transform our very existence.

Deep within the recesses of our minds, nestled like a precious gem, lies the amygdala. This tear-shaped structure, as identified by brilliant neuroscientists, serves as the pulsating heart of our emotional control. It eagerly absorbs the world around us, deciphering its every nuance, and orchestrating our body's response—be it the gentle embrace of sleep, the dance of digestion, or the fierce surge of fight-or-flight instincts. But emotions are not confined solely to the realm of biology; they possess a psychological dimension as well.

Sigmund Freud, the trailblazer of the human psyche, unearthed the profound truth that within each of us resides a tapestry of conscious and repressed emotions. These emotions, both known and hidden, shape the very fabric of our being, influencing our thoughts, actions, and aspirations. They are the untamed rivers of our souls, forever flowing and evolving.

But amidst this complex symphony of emotions, there lies a path to profound self-awareness and transformation—mindfulness. Across cultures and throughout the ages, wise souls have embraced the art of mindfulness, the practice of recognizing and accepting our emotions while remaining steadfast observers. Through this exquisite dance of self-awareness, we gain profound insights into the intricate workings of our bodies and minds.

With each brushstroke of emotion, we paint the masterpiece of our lives. The depth of our understanding and acceptance of our emotions empowers us to wield these colors with purpose and intention. We learn that even the so-called "negative" emotions hold vital lessons and serve as catalysts for growth and self-discovery. By embracing the full spectrum of our emotional experiences, we embark on a transformative journey toward self-realization.

Exercise: Tarot Emotions

Cards can be a valuable tool for associating emotions with various experiences. Choose your favorite card deck. Go through the deck and choose a card you like and a card you do not like. Consider the questions below while you contemplate those two cards.

What emotions are these cards provoking?

What is the origin of these emotions?

How has my family or community influenced my response to these cards?

What additional context do I need to know about these cards?

Do these emotions need to be neutralized? Why or why not?

What are my next steps, if any?

Affirmation

I allow my emotions to emerge, disappear, and rearrange as I heal and evolve.

SEEING ALL EMOTIONS WITH THE JUDGMENT CARD

Emotions are the raw essence of our humanity, coursing through our veins and shaping the very fabric of our existence. They have a profound impact on our lives, molding us into who we are and teaching us invaluable lessons along the way. When we shame ourselves for having certain emotions, we miss out on the messages our body is communicating to us about our inner workings. Emotions like anger, hatred, and jealousy offer valuable lessons that we miss out on when we ignore or suppress them. By getting curious about our emotions and understanding why we feel the way we do, we can learn more about ourselves and gain insight into our emotional experiences.

In many families, taboo emotions are often repressed, especially those associated with past trauma. But by allowing for healthy expressions of these emotions, we can navigate them in a productive way and use them as guides. This individual emotional regulation can also lead to collective emotional regulation within communities and societies, potentially reducing national tragedies and fostering the emergence of more emotionally aware political leaders.

Creating space for all emotions requires both personal choice and institutional design. Some societies prioritize positivity and view happiness, love, and godliness as the ultimate states to strive for. Others embrace the full spectrum of human emotions, recognizing that darkness and light coexist and contribute to our growth.

Similarly, tarot cards like Death and Judgment may evoke fear and discomfort due to their representation of endings and transformations. However, it is important to remember that these emotions are a natural part of being human. Instead of suppressing them, we should allow ourselves to fully experience and process them. Like the ebb and flow of the ocean tides, emotions come and go, and by embracing them, we can navigate life's challenges with resilience and self-awareness.

Ultimately, all emotions have value and can teach us valuable lessons. Rather than judging or avoiding them, we should strive to understand and accept them. By embracing the full range of human emotions, we can cultivate personal growth and become more empathetic and compassionate individuals.

Exercise: See Your Emotions

Scan your body.

Locate an emotion within you.

Decide whether to name the emotion.

Ask yourself, "What do I need to know about this emotion?"

Take inspired action, if you feel called to do so.

Affirmation

I give myself permission to fully embrace and honor all my emotions, knowing that they hold valuable messages for my growth and healing.

WITCH HUNTING WITH THE KING OF CUPS

Anyone who has used a deck of tarot cards is probably familiar with being ridiculed by those outside the practice, who view the use of symbols and archetypes outside of their normal experience as witchcraft. And in a sense, they're correct. But just because a practice is shunned as the other, doesn't mean it isn't effective or the answer to a long unanswered question.

Witches and witchcraft have a long and complex history, often shrouded in mystery and misunderstood by society. The Salem Witch Trials in the late 17th century serve as a vivid example of how societal fear and paranoia can lead to mass hysteria and the persecution of individuals. During this dark period, accusations of witchcraft were based on superstition and hearsay, rather than evidence or scientific understanding. Many innocent lives were lost. While our understanding of the natural world has since advanced, it is important to remain open-minded and acknowledge that there may still be phenomena or observations that defy scientific explanation, leaving room for the possibility that witches and their knowledge hold secrets that society has yet to fully recognize.

We can understand the use of tarot cards and visual images to tap into the subconscious through the lens of psychology and cognitive science. The human mind is incredibly complex and operates on both conscious and unconscious levels. Tarot cards, with their rich symbolism and archetypal imagery, have the potential to evoke deep emotions and activate neural pathways associated with memory, emotions, and intuitive thinking. When engaging with tarot, individuals may enter a state like meditation or focused attention, allowing for introspection and exploration of the subconscious mind. This practice aligns with the concept of symbolic cognition, where symbols and visual stimuli can trigger associations and insights from one's own personal experiences and beliefs. While the exact mechanisms are yet to be fully understood, the scientific explanation suggests that tarot cards and visual images can serve as powerful tools for self-reflection and accessing the deeper layers of the human psyche.

Many people have misconceptions about what tarot cards are and how they work. For example, when I say tarot, the modern person might picture a witchy woman in robes behind a dark curtain. But there is far more to tarot than that. In fact, tarot decks aren't even necessarily meant to predict futures (even though sometimes they can). They're supposed to reveal information within, including teaching you more about your Higher Self. There are very complex meanings in tarot decks, which is why becoming familiar with the symbolism and history of the cards is essential to having a healing conversation with a tarot mentor or guide.

To get more in sync with the link between your emotions and mind, consider how to witness your emotions in a tarot practice. This is helpful during times of burnout and exhaustion, especially if your symptoms manifest as common conditions like anxiety or depression.

Tarot Meditation: On Excommunication, Ghosting, and Cancelling with the King of Cups

Excommunication, or in modern culture, ghosting or cancelling, is an act of excluding individuals from a social or religious group. These behaviors cause intentional harm by triggering a profound nervous system response akin to the fight-or-flight mechanism. This response is rooted in our evolutionary biology and is designed to protect us from potential threats. When faced with the fear of being cast out or ostracized, our bodies instinctively prepare for survival. We can heal this response by making sure we always have a reservoir of self-love that we can draw from in the event someone's nervous system cannot handle additional relationship or interaction.

In this guided tarot meditation, we explore the transformative power of acceptance, and self-love through the themes of excommunication and the King of Cups.

Find a quiet space and take deep breaths to settle your mind.

Close your eyes and visualize standing in a sacred space surrounded by a calm ocean.

See the image of the King of Cups emerge from the water, holding compassion and love for self.

Reflect on being cancelled or excommunicated, allowing associated memories and emotions to surface without judgment.

Courageously invite the symbol or image of a time when you were cancelled or excommunicated to appear before you, see it, and feel it. Put your mind to it. Hold it close, send it love, and then release it from your hold.

Turn your attention back to the King of Cups, feeling his love and support envelop you.

Repeat affirmations of release, forgiveness, and worthiness.

Visualize the healing waters washing away excommunication, replacing it with healing and inner peace.

Bask in the freedom and integration of the King of Cups's energy, nurturing your emotional well-being.

Slowly return to the present moment, carrying the healing energy with you.

Through this tarot meditation, embrace forgiveness, self-acceptance, and emotional mastery. Release feelings of separation and connect with the healing waters of self-love and compassion as you continue your transformative journey.

Affirmation

I refuse to ghost, cancel, or excommunicate my self-care, self-love, and self-respect.

SCORPIO III: EMBRACING THE WILD WOMAN WITHIN

Seven of Cups as Venus in Scorpio

The wild woman embraces and integrates her raw feminine power—the power to seduce, attract, and create out of desire, wildness, and selfishness. Regardless of the externals, she remains devoted, beautiful, chaotic. Her body is tuned to the cycles of nature. The wild woman who embraces wildness as her truth is free to create her own boundaries—and she possesses wildness with the power to change the world.

THE MODERN-DAY WITCH TRIALS

Born in 1653 in Salem, Massachusetts, into an innkeeper's family, Sarah Good faced countless hardships and societal marginalization. Left penniless after legal disputes over her father's estate, she endured failed marriages that left her drowning in debt. By 1692, Sarah and her family were barely scraping by.

As a marginalized figure, Sarah became an easy target when rumors of witchcraft began circulating in Salem Village. Her reputation for being socially unpleasant, combined with her poverty, made her vulnerable. She was accused of afflicting two young girls with an unexplained illness that baffled medical practitioners of the time.

As fear and uncertainty gripped the community, the number of accusers grew. Throughout her trial, Sarah maintained her innocence, repeatedly proclaiming, "I am falsely accused." Yet, the community's fear, fueled by unexplained events and illnesses, prevailed over reason and fairness. Sarah was hanged as a "witch" on July 29, 1692.

You would think that modern society has evolved beyond this type of collective behavior.

Not quite.

In Suzanne O'Sullivan's book, *The Sleeping Beauties and Other Stories of Mystery Illness*, she recounts the tale of the "Witches of Le Roy" in 2011. A group of teenage girls experienced perplexing symptoms like severe twitching and verbal outbursts. The medical community initially struggled to find a physical cause for these symptoms. As more girls displayed similar signs and media attention grew, panic and confusion spread throughout the community. Eventually, the girls' condition was diagnosed as conversion disorder, a physical manifestation of psychological distress frequently associated with mass hysteria.

Both stories highlight how the fear of the unknown, coupled with unexplained phenomena can lead to mass hysteria and social isolation. When we don't understand something, it's human nature to try to make sense of it. In the absence of logical explanations, people often resort to superstition, blame, fear, or casual labeling of others on social media and in conversation as bipolar, narcissists, psychopaths, and the like. This labeling can quickly escalate into shunning others or a collective panic that overrides rational thought.

What we can learn from these stories is the importance of understanding and empathy. By doing so, we can help diffuse fear, prevent mass hysteria, and promote collective well-being. Let's strive to approach the unknown with curiosity, seeking knowledge instead of resorting to blame. Let's foster understanding and empathy, particularly when faced with things we don't immediately understand. Only then can we hope to prevent the repetition of such tragedies.

Remember, it's okay to seek help when grappling with unexplained symptoms or anxieties. Through seeking knowledge, practicing self-care, and cultivating a supportive community, we can navigate life's uncertainties with courage and resilience. In doing so, we transform our fears into opportunities for growth, understanding, and ultimately, healing.

Exercise: Heal with Your Inner Kitchen Witch

Connecting with your inner kitchen witch is a beautiful way to bring healing magic into your life. To begin, create a sacred space in your kitchen where you can connect with your inner witch. This could be a small altar or a designated area where you can grow herbs, prepare tinctures, and display meaningful items such crystals or candles. Next, spend time exploring the ingredients and tools in your kitchen. Engage all your senses as you touch, smell, taste, and observe the various elements. Connect with the energy of each ingredient and listen to your intuition as you choose what to use in your culinary creations. Embrace rituals such as blessing your meals, infusing them with intentions and gratitude. Keep a journal to record your experiences, insights, and any magical recipes you discover along the way.

Card Reflection: Standing Up Against Accusations

This tarot card spread will help you tap into your inner reservoir of strength to withstand the accusations of others who harm you because they cannot understand nor attempt to seek to understand your behavior.

Shuffle your deck and lay out ten cards side by side.

1. **The Accusation:** Reveals the nature and impact of the accusations against you.

2. **Inner Strength:** Reflects your resilience and ability to stay true to yourself.

3. **Self-Reflection:** Guides introspection and maintaining a positive self-image.

4. **Empowerment:** Identifies sources of support and empowerment.

5. **Protection:** Highlights methods to shield yourself from negativity.

6. **Truth and Clarity:** Helps discern truth from baseless accusations.

7. **Growth and Transformation:** Encourages personal development through adversity.

8. **Finding Support:** Points to those who can offer understanding and validation.

9. **Embracing Your Magic:** Celebrates your unique gifts and spiritual practices.

10. **Outcome:** Reveals potential resolution and growth from the experience.

Affirmation

I deserve love, acceptance, and understanding, regardless of others' misconceptions.

THE COMPLICATED SHADOW OF INDEPENDENCE WITH PLUTO

Pluto's archetype in astrology generally stands for transformation, power, and delving into the unconscious. It signifies rebirth, regeneration, and confronting our deepest fears and desires. Pluto represents the journey of self-discovery, where we confront our inner demons, shed outdated beliefs, and evolve into a more authentic version of ourselves. However, an excessive pursuit of independence can lead to self-destruction, serving as a cautionary tale for future generations about the importance of balance.

Consider the use of nuclear weaponry during World War II as an extreme example of this. The immense tension between nations led to destruction on an unprecedented scale, wiping out not just human lives but also causing irreversible environmental damage. Yet, in the wake of such devastation, there was a collective awakening. This led to the establishment of international peace-keeping organizations, non-proliferation agreements, and a global push toward nuclear disarmament.

In another historical context, Mary, Queen of Scots, pursued her ambitions with fierce independence, challenging established norms, which ultimately led to her martyrdom. However, her son, King James I, took a different route. He prioritized communal harmony over personal beliefs, bringing spiritual knowledge to the masses by translating the Bible into English, thus fostering unity and understanding.

When embarking on a healing journey, the newfound sense of independence and freedom can be exhilarating. Yet, it's vital to remember the lessons learned along the way and consider our impact on our community. As Eckhart Tolle points out in *A New Earth: Awakening to Your Life's Purpose*, while suffering is part of the human experience, unnecessary suffering—inflicted by humans onto each other—must be curtailed.

Independence is often seen as a symbol of strength and self-reliance. However, an overly independent mindset can isolate us, leading to unnecessary suffering. It can prevent us from seeking or accepting help, resulting in stress, loneliness, and burnout. True strength lies in knowing when to stand alone and when to seek support, creating a balance that encourages personal growth and community connection.

Exercise: Your Relationship with Independence

Find a quiet and comfortable space where you can reflect without distractions. Take a few deep breaths and center yourself. Begin by contemplating the following questions:

What does independence mean to you?

How has your pursuit of independence affected your relationships?

Have there been moments when you felt the weight of self-reliance?

Are there any fears or hesitations associated with relying on others?

Take your time to journal your thoughts and emotions, allowing yourself to delve into your experiences and insights.

Card Reflection: Cultivating Interdependence

Use this card spread to help you take intentional steps to cultivate interdependence in your life. Shuffle your deck and lay out four cards side by side.

1. Where can I seek opportunities to collaborate with others?

2. When do I need to practice deep listening while engaging in conversations with others?

3. When can I extend support to others without expecting anything in return?

4. Where can I create shared experiences and meaningful connections with others in my local geographic community?

Affirmation

I move between independence and connection, knowing both are essential for my healing.

THE DECANS OF SAGITTARIUS

Fire heals.

SAGITTARIUS I:
HEALING WITH FIRE

Eight of Wands as Mercury in Sagittarius

Healing requires fire. When we decide to live in the truth of who and what we are, we learn how to heal ourselves and our communities.

THE FIRE THAT DOESN'T BURN

Consider the sequoia trees, towering over 300 feet high and living for more than 2,000 years. As cone-bearing trees, they drop cones containing seeds that can remain dormant for thousands of years. Only with the aid of fire do these cones open to release their seeds, allowing them to germinate and grow into the magnificent trees they were destined to be.

Often, you witness forest fires—either directly or through media—and perceive it as a sign of the world's end due to climate change. Or you experience personal "fires" in your life, in the form of people, situations, or things that cause discomfort. You may believe that if only this "fire"—this person, circumstance, or object—were removed, your life would vastly improve. In the Christian tradition, hell is often depicted as a place of emptiness, darkness, and fire—a place you strive to avoid while clinging to the light of Jesus Christ.

However, by evading these metaphorical fires, you risk missing out on the lessons inherent in nature's design. These trials shape you into the person you might not want to be, but who society needs. Even Jesus had to descend into the void of the grave, and then hell, before he could be redeemed. This part of his journey is frequently overlooked. You might view Jesus's path of solitude and overcoming his inner demons as something beyond your own capabilities. Yet, fires are essential for growth. Just as fire enables the germination of sequoia seeds, so too does it ignite the dormant seeds within you. Sometimes, you might not even be aware of these seeds until they have fully bloomed.

It's during periods of burnout or adversity that your greatest strengths often emerge. By embracing these trials and developing resilience against the fire, you channel the savior you seek.

Exercise: Embracing the Fire Within

Take a moment to reflect on the metaphor of fire and its transformative power in your own life. Grab your journal and answer the following prompts:

Write about a recent experience that felt like a "fire" in your life. It could be a challenge, conflict, or adversity that you faced. How did you initially react to this "fire"? Did you try to avoid it, extinguish it, or embrace it? Explore your initial thoughts and feelings.

Reflect on any lessons or growth that emerged from this experience. What seeds within you were sparked by the fire? How did it shape and mold you into the person you are today?

Consider a current situation in your life where you may be resisting the fire—avoiding discomfort, conflict, or necessary change. What fears or beliefs are holding you back from fully embracing the transformative power of fire?

Visualize yourself stepping into the fire with courage and openness. What would it look like for you to lean into the discomfort and allow the fire to purify and ignite the seeds within you? Write down any insights or intentions that arise.

Card Reflection: Ignite Your Inner Fire

Shuffle your deck and lay out seven cards side by side.

1. **The Spark:** What is currently igniting the fire within you?

2. **Resistance and Fear:** What fears or beliefs are hindering your ability to work with fire?

3. **Purification:** How can you allow the fire to purify and release any stagnant energy?

4. **Embracing the Flames:** What steps can you take to courageously lean into the fire?

5. **Growth and Transformation:** What insights or opportunities for growth are emerging?

6. **Igniting Your Passion:** How can you channel the energy of the fire into a creative project?

7. **Inner Strength:** What inner resources or qualities can you tap into to support you?

Remember, the fire may be uncomfortable, but it holds the power to ignite your inner strength and bring forth your true potential. Embrace the flames, release resistance, and allow the fire to guide you toward growth, transformation, and healing.

Affirmation

I do not fear the fire. I am the fire.

BELIEVE IN LIGHT WHEN IT IS DARK, BELIEVE IN DARK WHEN IT IS LIGHT

Your life is a complex tapestry of emotions, experiences, and viewpoints, where straightforward "good" and "bad" or "light" and "dark" often don't fully capture its rich depth. Grasping this, you step into the sphere of duality, an idea that accepts the coexistence of seemingly contrary elements within you and everything around you.

As you enter the first decan of Sagittarius, you find yourself in a season when the Northern Hemisphere globally starts shifting its gaze from the encroaching darkness to the anticipation of light's return. Meanwhile, in the Southern Hemisphere, many are basking in the height of the light season, their days lengthening while their nights shorten. Even if all you perceive is darkness, remember, the light is there, even if it's not immediately visible.

The centaur, a mythical entity with the torso of a human and the lower body of a horse, serves as a powerful emblem of this duality. It combines both primal instincts (embodied by the horse) and intellectual prowess (represented by the human), blending light and dark, strength and fragility, wisdom and folly, and the left and right hemispheres of your brain. The centaur's dual nature provides a reflection of your own intricate existence, underscoring that welcoming both light and dark can guide you toward a fulfilling life.

You, like everyone else, will face periods of illness, darkness, or difficulty. During these times, maintaining faith in the existence of light—hope, joy, love—may seem daunting. However, it's precisely in these moments that clinging to the light becomes paramount.

On the other hand, during phases of joy and prosperity, acknowledging the existence of darkness—fear, doubt, sadness—can keep you anchored. Understanding that life's highs and lows are equally significant for your growth allows you to savor your triumphs while also equipping you for potential obstacles.

Exercise: Exploring Duality with Ashes

The concept of duality forms the bedrock of human experience. It's the idea that two seemingly opposing forces can coexist and influence each other, much like light and dark, joy and sorrow, or creation and destruction. This exercise using ashes—a symbol of both endings (destruction) and potential for new beginnings (creation)—will provide a unique way to explore this concept.

Step 1: Gather Your Ashes. Find ashes from any source—it could be from a fireplace, a burnt letter, or incense. The source isn't as important as the symbolism they hold.

Step 2: Find a Quiet Place. Find a quiet, peaceful place where you won't be disturbed. This could be in your home, a garden, or a park. Make yourself comfortable and take a few moments to breathe deeply and center yourself.

Step 3: Observe the Ashes. Hold the ashes in your hands. Observe their texture, color, and smell. Think about their origin— once something whole, now reduced to ashes. But also consider their potential—ashes often enrich soil, giving life to new plants.

Step 4: Reflect on Duality. As you hold the ashes, reflect on the dual nature they represent—destruction and creation. Ask yourself these questions:

How have I experienced this duality in my own life?

What parts of me have been "burned down" to make way for new growth?

How can I embrace both the destructive and creative forces within me?

Remember, there's no right or wrong answers here. Allow any emotions or thoughts that arise to flow freely. This process may trigger feelings of sadness, joy, regret, or hope. These are all part of your personal journey of exploration and understanding.

Step 5: Release the Ashes. When you're ready, release the ashes. You may wish to scatter them in your garden, in a body of water, or let the wind carry them away. As you do so, envision releasing any resistance you might have toward the dualities within you.

After the exercise, continue to ponder upon these ideas. You might choose to journal your thoughts or discuss them with others. Applying this understanding to your interactions can enhance empathy, as you'll appreciate the complex interplay of opposites within everyone.

Remember, exploring duality is an ongoing journey, not a destination. Regularly repeating this exercise can offer new insights as you navigate different stages of your life. Embrace the process and watch your understanding of yourself and the world around you.

Card Reflection: Embrace Your Inner Centaur

Just as the centaur unifies two distinct aspects, we too can integrate our own dualities. Embracing our strengths and weaknesses, our triumphs and failures, our light and dark, enables us to navigate life with grace and wisdom. To begin, visualize yourself as a centaur. Contemplate its strength, agility, and wisdom, and how these qualities reflect within you.

Shuffle your deck and lay out five cards side by side.

1. Recognize your light—your strengths, achievements, and joy.

2. Acknowledge your dark—your areas of growth, setbacks, and fears.

3. How do these elements conflict?

4. How do these elements complement each other?

5. How can you create a harmonious balance between the two?

Affirmation

Like the changing seasons, I welcome the cycles of light and dark in my life, understanding they are part of my human experience.

BURNING FIRST IMPRESSIONS

In our society, it is all too easy to judge people solely based on their outward appearances. However, true understanding and connection can only be achieved when we see beyond superficial traits and recognize everyone as a unique person with their own stories, their own karma, and their own goals, wishes and dreams that we may be able to support.

"Home Alone," the 1990 comedy classic, cleverly weaves a tale that transcends the slapstick humor and holiday cheer to deliver a potent message about forgiveness and repentance. At the center of this narrative is young Kevin McCallister, who evolves from a brash and petulant child into a compassionate and understanding individual. His transformation is catalyzed by his interactions with the elderly neighbor, a character initially portrayed as menacing but later revealed to be a lonely, misunderstood man burdened by his past mistakes and estranged relationship with his daughter. Their relationship underscores the power of overcoming fear and prejudice to find common ground.

Kevin's journey toward forgiveness is not just about pardoning others, but also about self-forgiveness and learning from his own mistakes. The film subtly incorporates the concept of fate, suggesting that Kevin was destined to be left behind to confront his fears and grow from the experience. Faith plays a crucial role in the narrative, not necessarily in a religious sense, but as a faith in the goodness in people, and the potential for change and redemption and how the Universe can orchestrate individual "mistakes" that turn to become collective "blessings." It emphasizes the idea that everyone deserves a second chance, a message that, if embraced, can foster empathy and compassion within society.

Exercise: Creating Inclusive Spaces

During certain seasons of life, it can be easy to fall into an us versus them mentality, excluding others to protect our own or our tribe. Someone may not celebrate or remember in the same way we do, and instead of appreciating the way they celebrate, we shun them and label them as the other. To combat prejudices and biases, it is crucial to create environments where individuals can express their true selves without fear of judgment or exclusion. Here are some ways we can accomplish this:

Encourage diversity and inclusion: Celebrate and value different perspectives, talents, and backgrounds in your personal and professional circles.

Challenge discriminatory behavior: Speak out against prejudice and bias whenever you encounter it, promoting a culture of inclusivity.

Support marginalized voices: Amplify the stories and experiences of individuals who are often overlooked or silenced, ensuring their voices are heard.

Together, we can create a more inclusive and compassionate society where everyone's true selves are celebrated and valued.

Affirmation

Like fire, I purify and refine, letting go of what no longer serves me and making space for new opportunities.

SAGITTARIUS II: AUTHENTIC FORGIVENESS

Nine of Wands as Moon in Sagittarius

I am who I am because I choose who I am. But I am who I am because I didn't choose too. Your freedom is bound up in mine.

JOSEPH'S EXAMPLE OF AUTHENTIC FORGIVENESS

In the Jewish tradition, Joseph's story from the Torah begins with a young man growing up in an agrarian community. He was favored by his father, but his brothers harbored deep resentment toward him. Their jealousy led to Joseph being sold into slavery, ultimately leading to his rise in prominence within the great empire of Egypt. However, unbeknownst to Joseph's brothers, future events would unfold, changing the dynamics of their relationships.

Years later, Joseph's family faced a dire famine in their land. Lacking the preparedness of the mighty Egyptian empire, they turned to the city for help, unknowingly seeking assistance from none other than their long-lost brother Joseph—the very same person they had callously sold into slavery years ago.

While revenge may have been a natural inclination for many in Joseph's position, he took a different path. He forgave his brothers fully, focusing not on what was best for himself, but on what was best for society at-large. With unwavering faith, Joseph entrusted the ultimate verdict to a higher power, declaring, "Am I in the place of God? You intended evil toward me, but God intended it for good, to bring about the saving of many lives. Therefore, do not be afraid. I will nourish you and your children."

What's interesting about this story is that Joseph did not require his brothers to apologize. He merely did what was best for everyone involved, under the specific facts of the situation, and left the rest to work it out for itself.

Joseph's extraordinary act of forgiveness in the face of betrayal teaches us valuable lessons about the transformative power of letting go and embracing a higher perspective. By releasing resentment, focusing on the greater good, and trusting in divine order, we can embark on a journey of personal growth, healing, and reconciliation.

Exercise: Healing Resentment

Sometimes resentment must be worked through on the path to full forgiveness. Take a moment to reflect and journal on the following:

1. Identify Resentment Triggers: Take a moment to reflect on specific situations or individuals that consistently trigger feelings of resentment within you. It could be related to relationships, work, or any aspect of your life that causes emotional discomfort.

2. Journal Your Thoughts: Grab a journal and write down these incidents or unresolved issues. This act of putting your thoughts on paper allows for a sense of release and clarity.

3. Reflect on Your Emotions: Dive into each recorded event and identify the negative emotions associated with them. Is it anger, disappointment, frustration? Acknowledge these feelings without judgment.

4. Differentiate Controllable and Uncontrollable Factors: Consider which aspects of these situations you have the power to change, and which ones are beyond your control. By doing so, you gain perspective and can focus your energy on what is within your sphere of influence.

5. Develop an Action Plan: For the controllable factors, create an action plan. Determine the steps you can take to address these issues, such as having a conversation, setting boundaries, or seeking support from others.

6. Visualize Forgiveness: Shift your focus to the uncontrollable factors and practice visualizing forgiveness. Imagine yourself letting go of the resentment, freeing yourself from its burden, and opening up space for healing and growth.

7. Embrace Patience and Persistence: Recognize that forgiveness is a process that takes time. Be patient with yourself as you work through these emotions and persist in practicing forgiveness, even when it feels challenging.

By engaging in this exercise regularly, you can cultivate a mindset of forgiveness and release the weight of resentment. Remember, forgiveness is not about condoning or forgetting past hurts, but about reclaiming your own emotional well-being.

Affirmation

I choose to focus on the present moment, releasing the past and embracing a future of forgiveness.

WHEN YOU'RE NOT READY TO FORGIVE WITH TEMPERANCE AND THE WHEEL OF FORTUNE

In addition to the story of Joseph, the Jewish tradition encompasses four sequential stories that revolve around the theme of sibling rivalry. These tales include Cain and Abel, Issac and Ishmael, Jacob and Esau, and finally, Joseph and his brothers. Through this progression, we witness a spectrum of relationship dynamics, ranging from fratricide to coexistence.

The story of Cain and Abel portrays a competition set up by the Divine, where the two brothers are asked to present offerings. Cain diligently offers the best fruits of his labor, while Abel chooses to offer a sheep from his flock. The Divine recognizes Abel's offering, which ignites Cain's rage. In his anger, he commits fratricide, failing to grasp the limits of his own power. Consequently, Cain is banished from the land, revealing the consequences of his inability to understand his own abilities.

According to Rabbi Lord Jonathan Sacks, this narrative, along with others in the Torah, convey two profound messages about creating a harmonious and peaceful world. Firstly, families form the foundation of society and the state. If individuals cannot resolve conflict and practice forgiveness within their smallest units, stable societies and cohesive nations cannot thrive. Secondly, broken families have political consequences. Rabbi Sacks cites the defeat and exile of Israel following periods of intense factionalism and internal strife as examples.

Although forgiveness is not always easy and may take time, it is essential for our healing journey. Without forgiveness, wounds remain open and cannot fully heal. By embracing forgiveness, we can move forward and experience true healing and growth. Ultimately, we are all people, and while there are always exceptions to the rule of forgiveness, the exceptions are less frequent than we may think.

Exercise: Repairing Family Relationships

Recall personal experiences of family rivalry and conflict, as well as moments of forgiveness.

Analyze the themes and lessons from stories like Cain and Abel, Isaac and Ishmael, Jacob and Esau, and Joseph and his brothers.

Consider emotions toward family and any unresolved conflicts.

Explore the meaning of forgiveness and identify barriers to forgiveness.

Plan steps toward resolution and strategies for practicing forgiveness.

Envision a future where forgiveness strengthens family relationships.

Set goals for nurturing and improving relationships with family.

Remember, this exercise aims to promote self-reflection, healing, and understanding through forgiveness in family relationships. Take your time and be honest with yourself. Work with professionals or mediators where necessary. Forgiveness is a journey that some may not take with you. Be open to doing the best you can with what you have in the present moment and give the Universe space to work the rest.

Card Reflection: Forgiveness

Shuffle your deck and lay out ten cards side by side.

1. **The Past:** What events or emotions have led to the need for forgiveness?

2. **Release:** What resentment, anger, and hurt associated with the situation can you release?

3. **Understanding:** What additional insight do you need to foster empathy and compassion?

4. **Healing:** How can you heal yourself through self-care and forgiveness of oneself?

5. **Reconciliation:** Is reconciliation desirable and can trust and harmony be rebuilt?

6. **Transformation:** This card signifies the positive changes and growth that forgiveness can bring. Embrace the potential for personal transformation and a renewed sense of self.

7. **Boundaries:** This card reminds you to establish healthy boundaries moving forward. Consider what boundaries are necessary to protect yourself and maintain a balanced relationship.

8. **Acceptance:** This card represents accepting the past and the reality of the situation. Embrace acceptance as a step toward forgiveness and peace.

9. **Gratitude:** This card signifies finding gratitude amidst forgiveness. Reflect on the lessons learned and

the opportunities for growth that have arisen from the experience.

10. **Moving Forward:** This card represents the path ahead after forgiveness. Consider how you can use this experience as a catalyst for positive change and creating healthier relationships.

Affirmation

Forgiveness heals me through by freeing energy stuck in my body in the form of grudges.

GIVING AND RECEIVING FEEDBACK WITH THE KNIGHT OF WANDS

Having the ability to give and receive feedback is an essential part of the forgiveness process. It is how we negotiate boundaries within a relationship that we are intent on preserving. Usually in the best negotiations, everyone gives up a little so we can all coexist in harmony. Unless you were raised in a family where giving and receiving feedback in a systematic, heart-and-mind way was the norm (most of us weren't), giving and receiving feedback is a skill that must be developed over time.

While a structure for giving feedback in a peer-to-peer way was discussed during the decans of Libra, Sagittarius focuses on giving feedback in situations when there is a hierarchy of knowledge— someone has more education or experience than another—but we want to give feedback in a way that honors both parties as humans.

Giving and receiving feedback is both a science and art. One of the best ways to practice and to create an environment open to feedback is to incorporate feedback giving and receiving into already-existing routines. When I worked in the public school system, we had countless opportunities to give and receive feedback. This included weekly one-on-one check-ins, where we shared strengths and areas of growth with not only the people we managed but those who managed us, and daily power-up and powerdowns, where we reflected on the micro-challenges and successes of the day. But when I moved to teach at different schools, and then eventually changed careers, I realized that this wonderful culture of feedback was the exception, not the rule.

Many of us do not have the opportunity to participate in a growth-oriented culture—one focused on holding space for challenges and that lets you receive challenges through the delivery of feedback. When we fail to see feedback as a gift, we see it as an affront—a challenge to our character, a place where we are not accepted as we'd like to be accepted. We stew in the negative comments, disrespect, and gossip.

But we must also remember that it is our choice to allow the opinions of others to dictate the emotion we're feeling. Even when we have an involuntary emotional response, we can always engage the mind to reorient our emotions to the direction we'd rather head in. Sometimes that means acting in accordance with someone's feedback. Sometimes it means noticing someone's feedback is not for you while still acknowledging it. Either way, you are not what other people say you are. You are who the Universe says you are. Choose to not get offended, even when your first response is to be offended. Choose to stay in your peace. Choose to stay in joy.

There will always be people who don't see your perspective. And that's okay. Stay in agreement with the Universe. Be responsive, not reactive, to the words of others.

Tarot Meditation: Giving and Receiving Feedback with the Knight of Wands

Visualize a figure approaching you on horseback. It is the Knight of Wands, representing the spirit of adventure and inspiration. Notice the fiery energy that radiates from their armor and the wand they hold in their hand. This knight comes to invite you to reflect on how you offer and receive feedback in your life.

Take a moment to connect with your inner wisdom. Ask yourself: How can I offer feedback constructively? How can I receive feedback with an open heart and mind?

Now, imagine a bright light shining from the knight's wand, illuminating the path before you. This light represents healing, compassionate, and constructive feedback. It holds the power to guide you toward growth and development.

As you continue to soak in the energy of the Knight of Wands, think about a situation where you would like to deliver feedback to another person. Reflect on the following tips for giving feedback in a healing and compassionate manner. Observe in non-judgment any emotions or thoughts that come up.

Start with a positive intention: Remember that the purpose of feedback is to help someone grow and improve. Imagine yourself approaching the conversation with the intention of supporting their development rather than criticizing or judging. Be specific and objective: Clearly articulate the behavior or situation you are providing feedback on. Imagine having a fact-based conversation that avoids generalizations or personal attacks. Use "I" statements: Imagine sharing your own observations and experiences using "I" statements, which convey your perspective without sounding accusatory or confrontational. This encourages open dialogue and understanding.

Offer suggestions for improvement: Imagine instead of focusing solely on what went wrong, providing constructive suggestions for how the person can enhance their skills or approach. Hear yourself offering concrete examples or resources that can assist them in their growth journey.

Now, shift your focus to receiving feedback with grace and openness. Remember that feedback is an opportunity for growth and self-reflection. Consider the following questions:

How can you focus on the message itself rather than how it was delivered? Even if the tone or delivery may be challenging to hear, how can you try to extract the valuable insights and set aside any emotional reactions?

How can you pause and seek to understand instead of immediately responding to the feedback? Are there any underlying patterns or areas for improvement that you can identify?

How can you choose your response to feedback with intention? When will you accept? When will you reject? When will you reconsider? Remember that feedback is a gift; you don't have to use all gifts, but it is gracious to receive it. When considering what you want to do with the feedback, ask yourself: Does this feedback resonate with me and align with my values? Does it offer valuable insights for my growth? Trust your intuition and decide which option serves your development best.

As you open your eyes and return to the present moment, carry the wisdom of the Knight of Wands with you. Embrace feedback as a catalyst for growth and positive change. Approach both giving and receiving feedback with an open heart and mind, knowing that it is an integral part of your healing journey.

Affirmation

I embrace the power of feedback as a gift, knowing that it has the potential to heal and transform both the giver and the receiver.

SAGITTARIUS III:
A SEASON FOR EVERYTHING

Ten of Wands as Saturn in Sagittarius

What once was bearable becomes unbearable when we keep it beyond its time. To everything there is a season—a season for carrying and a season for letting go. A season for dark, a season for light. A season where we realize that burnout, although challenging, can be used as a springboard to create a more desirable life.

FREEDOM REQUIRES BOUNDARIES

We commonly associate Sagittarius with freedom, travel, and expansion. But we fail to remember that Sagittarius is ruled by Jupiter, who also represents the law and the institutions that uphold the law. This makes sense. Many people associate the god Zeus with Jupiter. While being associated with a god has its advantages, it also means you must set boundaries with others to ensure your freedoms are protected.

In short, freedom exists within boundaries. When we do not have boundaries, we are not free. A cosmos with Jupiter but no Saturn gives us a Universe where there is all gas and no brake.

I saw this when I was a classroom teacher. Many first-year teachers think the cool thing to do is *not* set expectations and *not* set rules. They think the kids will learn to love them and have fun with all the "cool" activities they do. But what ends up happening is that kids perform poorly on the very exams necessary to achieve their goals. Or if they don't care about their exams, they fail to learn the character lessons they need to become the person they want to become. Many students also become codependent on the teacher—acting in ways to get the teacher to like them, instead of interdependent *with* the teacher, meaning they respect the teacher for their ancestral wisdom while also offering their youthful perspective as well.

The most impactful teachers (and ultimately most recognized teachers) are those long-term ones who may be hated at the beginning but whom the kids learned to respect. These teachers held high expectations for behavior but were also there to have fun after school. They cared about being a mentor for the kids more than being liked. They were firm, fair, consistent, and fun.

There is a time for learning and a time for play. We cannot always play, because then we miss opportunities to learn. We cannot always learn, because then we miss opportunities to explore.

Freedom without limits is not freedom at all—it's chaos. If you enjoy chaos, that's okay too. But when we live our lives in chaos, we become subject to its whims, when we should be creating a life on our terms. If a life subjected to the whims of others is what you want, that's valid. But I think many of us prefer to live life on our own terms, instead of the terms of others.

Exercise: Choosing Boundaries

Choosing boundaries is a proactive step to healing and personal growth. Proactive boundaries are the limits we choose to set in our relationships and interactions with others, be it at work, within our families, or in our intimate partnerships. They serve as a means of asserting our needs, values, and personal space while also establishing a framework for respectful and healthy communication.

To identify, set, and enforce boundaries in a self-compassionate way, consider your needs, values, and personal limits. Self-awareness plays a crucial role in understanding what feels uncomfortable or draining in various situations. It is essential to validate and honor these feelings without judgment.

Communicating boundaries involves expressing oneself clearly and assertively, using "I" statements to convey personal needs and expectations. It is important to remember that setting boundaries might require practice and adjustment over time, as relationships and circumstances evolve. Clients are supported in developing strategies for effectively enforcing boundaries and managing potential conflicts or pushback, ensuring their boundaries are respected.

Affirmation

I release the need to please others at the expense of my own well-being, knowing that my worth does not depend on their approval.

SOFTENING THE MIND AND OPENING THE HEART TO FORGIVE WITH THE SOLSTICES

There are things many of us have been holding on to for far too long. Be it an injustice, a hurt, a time when someone did us wrong. We hold on to all the times when we feel like we should have had a different experience. Consider whether you want to continue holding on to that pain, that injustice, that hurt, or if you'd rather let it go and trust the Universe to make it up to you.

Forgiveness can feel impossible. The injustice is too great to just "get over." The inequalities are too unfair to just "let it go." The pain is too much to just "leave in the past." But the thing that we must remember is that forgiveness is not about the other person—it's about protecting our own energy.

When we fail to forgive, we choose to allow the pain of the past to continue to affect our present. This affects the choices we make, while the person who caused the injustice continues to live their life. Holding on to injustice and pain or seeking revenge keeps us stuck in a cycle of repair and breakdown, rather than one of healing and creation. When you decide to forgive someone— whether it be a politician, spouse, or friend—you lay down your burdens. And you realize you can set yourself free.

Forgiveness does not mean you won't have scars. Just because you forgive someone, doesn't mean there isn't a scar. It doesn't mean that the laws shouldn't be changed. It doesn't mean the behavior should continue. All forgiveness means is that you are allowing yourself to choose where you direct your energy instead of allowing someone else's actions to dictate your life.

We all have visions and goals for our lives. Don't allow another person to keep you from moving forward. The energy you expend to pay people back is energy that could be spent creating a new world for others.

Holding on to hurt will consume your thoughts and hopes of a better future. It's like a wound that keeps being reopened. Give it time to heal. Forgive, and then allow the healing process to take root. And when there is a scar, all it means is that you have a story to share with others.

Exercise: Ritualizing Renewal and Forgiveness with the Winter Solstice

In the realm of astrology, solstice points hold a significant place, serving as celestial markers that influence our connection with the cosmos. These pivotal moments mark the extreme points of the sun's journey through the zodiac, where it reaches its highest (summer solstice) and lowest (winter solstice) points in the sky. In this article, we delve into the profound significance of the winter solstice, exploring its astrological and spiritual importance, while offering guidance on how to harness its energy for personal growth and reflection.

As the days grow shorter and colder, the winter solstice brings forth a moment of great significance in the yearly cycle. Falling on or around December 21 in the Northern Hemisphere, it marks the shortest day and longest night of the year. In astrological terms, the sun enters Capricorn, heralding a period of introspection and inner transformation.

Working with the Winter Solstice: To tap into the transformative energies of the winter solstice, consider incorporating rituals, meditations, and practices that align with this sacred time. Here are some suggestions:

Setting the Stage: Choose a quiet and serene space where you can be undisturbed. Create an ambiance that fosters introspection, such as lighting candles or using soft, soothing music. Consider adorning your space with symbols of rebirth and renewal, like evergreen branches or crystals. Morning Meditation: Rise early to witness the first light of the day, symbolizing the return of the Sun's strength. Find a comfortable position, close your eyes, and focus on your breath. Visualize the warming rays of the rising sun infusing you with renewed energy and vitality. Set intentions for the coming year, focusing on personal growth, forgiveness, and releasing old patterns.

Solstice Ritual of Forgiveness: Write down any grudges, resentments, or emotional burdens that you wish to release. Take a moment to reflect on the pain they have caused you and the weight they have carried in your life. Then, one by one, offer forgiveness to those who have wronged you, including yourself. As you burn or bury these written representations, visualize the release of negative energy, making space for healing and renewal.

Nature Connection: Spending time in nature is a powerful way to honor the winter solstice's symbolism of rebirth. Take a mindful walk in the crisp winter air, observing the sleeping plants and trees. Connect with the stillness and embrace the opportunity for inner reflection. Consider journaling your thoughts and insights as you commune with nature.

Affirmation

Forgiveness is a gift I give to myself, allowing me to move forward with grace and resilience.

THE DECANS OF CAPRICORN

In the dark
Begins a labor
Without glamour
Producing Pressure
Required
For Diamonds
To Form

CAPRICORN I: BUILDING FROM THE GROUND UP

Two of Pentacles as Jupiter in Capricorn

As our healing proceeds, we start integrating repaired parts of ourselves into our new reality. The road to recovery might be veiled in mystery, yet we forge ahead with courage. While our journey may bring us full circle back to our starting point, we will not be the same. Our perspective will have evolved. The process of healing has reshaped us, enabling us to perceive our original state through a lens of transformation and growth.

SATURN RETURNS AS THE DEVIL

As we step into the embrace of Capricorn season, we find ourselves at an equinox point, where Earth's tilt redirects our path. This celestial movement ushers in a profound sense of boundaries and limitations. Our existence is intricately woven within the fabric of specific conditions, marked by two polar extremes. Some may liken it to an upper and lower range, while others perceive it as an oscillation between two points, each accompanied by its own unique resistance.

In astrology, Saturn takes center stage as the planet synonymous with boundaries, restrictions, and the wisdom of age. It embodies the eternal dance between light and darkness, duality and balance, linear and nonlinear time. Occupying the outermost sphere in traditional astrology, Saturn acts as a mediator between the inner and outer planets. It holds space for chronos time, the familiar linear time defined by clocks and calendars, in contrast to kairos time, the cyclical and infinite concept of time without beginning or end.

This dance between chronos and kairos permeates every facet of our lives, particularly during the significant phase known as the "Saturn return." This pivotal period occurs when Saturn completes its orbit and returns to the position it held at the time of our birth, as indicated in our natal charts. The Saturn return is renowned for bringing confusion and tests our way, serving as a checkpoint to gauge how we are navigating the karmic lessons from both past and present lives.

Approximately every 30 years, the Saturn return graces our lives (though individual variations exist based on natal charts). It stands as a crucial juncture demanding our attention. During this transformative time, profound shifts often occur—career transformations, relationship metamorphoses, and other profound changes that shape our very existence. By cultivating awareness, presence, and surrendering to the preparations for this celestial return, we enhance our ability to navigate these sometimes-turbulent waters with grace, rather than being swept away by the waves of change.

Exercise: A Time to Reflect on Time

Reflect on the concept of time. Write about your experience with chronos time—the linear progression of minutes, hours, and days. Consider any challenges or stressors it presents. Then, explore kairos time—moments where time stands still, when you're fully present and engaged. Reflect on the impact of both on your well-being. Practice mindfulness to cultivate awareness of both types of time. Set intentions to prioritize meaningful moments and create a healthier balance. Embrace a more balanced approach for greater fulfillment and mindfulness in the present moment.

Card Reflection: Saturn Return

For this Saturn return spread, shuffle your deck and lay out six cards side by side.

1. **The Past:** Draw a card that represents the lessons learned during your last Saturn return (if applicable).

2. **The Present:** Draw a card to reflect the current challenges and transformations occurring in your life due to the Saturn return.

3. **Lessons to Learn:** Draw a card that signifies the lessons and growth expected from this Saturn return.

4. **Future Changes:** Draw a card to symbolize potential changes or developments to expect.

5. **Action Steps:** Draw a card to indicate actionable steps to take during this transitional period.

6. **Outcome:** Draw a final card to represent the overall outcome or result of this Saturn return.

Affirmation

I am open to the lessons that my Saturn returns teach me.

WISDOM AS THE ANTIDOTE TO THE POISONED APPLE

Apples have a rich history steeped in symbolism and mythology within various cultures. Take, for example, the biblical tale of Adam and Eve, where the apple from the Tree of Knowledge represents temptation and the pursuit of wisdom, leading to profound consequences. Interestingly, the iconic Apple phone logo features a bitten apple, which some interpret as a subtle reference to this biblical story, symbolizing the boundless access to knowledge and the disruptive power of technology in our modern era.

In today's fast-paced world, we find ourselves inundated with an overwhelming amount of information, much like a seductive yet potentially harmful poisoned apple. The effects of excessive knowledge can leave us feeling bewildered and disconnected.

Without the necessary tools for discernment, we risk getting lost in a labyrinth of facts, opinions, and misinformation.

The initial step toward detoxifying ourselves from this overload is to embrace the practice of mindfulness. By staying fully present and focused, we can filter out irrelevant information and regain the clarity needed to engage our discernment and lead us toward the path of wisdom.

Wisdom is the profound understanding gained through knowledge and experience, empowering us to make sound judgments and informed choices. As our knowledge and experiences grow, we become more adept at recognizing patterns across different contexts, unveiling common truths that fine-tune our intuition. On the other hand, discernment is the ability to perceive and differentiate between various options, evaluating their value and authenticity. At times, we may encounter ideas that appear equally valid. Discernment allows us to determine what is consistently true, occasionally true, or never true. Wisdom fuels discernment by enabling us to navigate the nuances of a world that exists in shades of gray, and once we embrace these shades of gray, in all the vivid colors of the rainbow.

Exercise: Working with the Apple to Connect to Wisdom

Throughout history, the apple has held a significant place in human culture. From ancient times to modern symbolism, it has been revered for its symbolic value, spiritual associations, and connection to wisdom. In this exercise, we will explore the rich history and spiritual uses of the apple while cultivating wisdom and discernment.

Step 1: Reflect on Past Experiences

In ancient mythology, the apple was often associated with immortality, knowledge, temptation, and fertility. Think about past events that resonate with the essence of the apple. What type of memories do you usually link with this fruit? Evaluate the advantages or disadvantages of cultivating more, fewer, or different connections with the symbol of the apple.

Step 2: Embrace Mindfulness with the Apple

Take an apple in your hand and appreciate its physical presence. Feel its smoothness, weight, and shape. Engage in a moment of mindfulness, allowing yourself to be fully present with the apple. Let go of distractions and immerse yourself in the sensory experience. Consider the statement and what it brings up for you, *"I give myself permission to limit exposure to information that causes stress or overwhelm."*

Step 3: Engage in Critical Thinking with the Apple

The apple has been a symbol of knowledge and enlightenment throughout history. Contemplate a topic or issue of interest to you. Write down relevant facts, opinions, and arguments related to this topic on apple-shaped notes. Engage in critical thinking, considering sources, biases, and potential implications of each viewpoint.

Step 4: Explore Spiritual Uses of the Apple

The apple has also been used in various spiritual practices as a means to connect with wisdom and insight. Research different spiritual traditions or beliefs that incorporate the apple into their rituals or symbolism. Take note of any teachings or practices that resonate with you on a deeper level.

Step 5: Apply Wisdom with the Apple

Consider a current decision or dilemma you are facing. Utilize the insights gained from your critical thinking and spiritual exploration to evaluate each option. Allow the symbolism and spiritual significance of the apple to guide your discernment process. Trust your intuition and inner wisdom as you make your decision.

Step 6: Reflect and Adjust with the Apple

After making your decision, take time to reflect on the outcome. Consider whether your choice aligned with your values and the wisdom you sought. If necessary, adjust your approach and continue refining your connection to wisdom and discernment in future decisions.

As you continue on this journey, remember the profound symbolism and spiritual significance that the apple holds. Embrace its wisdom and let it guide you toward a deeper understanding of yourself and the choices you make.

Card Reflection: The Seeker

Draw one tarot card. This card represents you as "The Seeker." The Seeker card reminds you to remain curious and open-minded. Embrace the thirst for knowledge and seek answers from various sources. Just like The Seeker, be fearless in venturing into unexplored territories and exploring different perspectives. Trust your intuition as you navigate through the vast sea of information. Remember that every piece of knowledge you acquire contributes to your personal growth. Stay true to your quest for truth and wisdom, and let this card guide you on this enlightening path.

Affirmation

I cultivate a healthy balance between staying informed and preserving my mental well-being.

CAPRICORN II: CREATIVE POWER

Three of Pentacles as Mars in Capricorn

Embrace your innate capacity as a creator. To be fruitful and multiply is to contribute to the rich tapestry of life with our unique insights, talents, and visions. It's to foster innovation, to birth new concepts, and to shape the world in ways yet unimagined. It is about fostering a growth mindset, embracing change, and continuously seeking opportunities to learn, innovate and improve.

CREATION DOESN'T ALWAYS MEAN MAKING BABIES

In Napoleon Hill's timeless classic, *Think and Grow Rich,* the author explores the profound concept of the Mystery of Sex Transmutation. While the title may initially evoke thoughts solely related to human sexuality, the underlying theme extends far beyond that limited scope.

Hill reminds us that sex desire is one of the most powerful human desires, but it goes beyond physical expression. When we learn how to transmute creative energy from the limbic mind to the critical mind, and learn how to connect the two at will, we can unlock its potential for other creative endeavors. By aligning ourselves with this force and channeling our creative energy, we infuse our projects with vitality and passion. It teaches us to cultivate intense desires, using the burning desire for success, power, or the realization of our dreams as fuel to transmute our creative energy into actions that propel us toward our goals.

Embracing the infinite potential contained within our creative energy, we open ourselves to exploring limitless possibilities for growth, innovation, and contribution to the world. The Mystery of Sex Transmutation reminds us that creating life encompasses a vast spectrum of possibilities beyond human reproduction.

Ultimately, this concept encourages us to become co-creators of our own lives. It invites us to transmute our creative energy into actions, ideas, and experiences that enrich not only our own existence but also the world around us.

Exercise: Be Fruitful and Multiply

This journal exercise will guide you in exploring ways to multiply in quality, skill, and the ability to address societal needs. By embracing this holistic interpretation, you can make a positive impact on the world around you.

Reflect on personal growth: Begin by contemplating areas of your life where you can multiply in quality. Ask yourself: What are my strengths and talents? How can I nurture and refine them further? Write down at least three areas where you would like to multiply in quality.

Expand your abilities: Think about the skills and abilities that can empower you to contribute more effectively to your communities. Identify areas where you can develop expertise to address societal challenges. Write down specific skills or abilities you would like to cultivate or improve upon.

Multiply in compassion and empathy: Now, shift your focus to multiplying in compassion, empathy, and love toward others. Reflect on the relationships in your life and evaluate how you can foster stronger connections. Write down three ways in which you can multiply in compassion and empathy toward others.

Collaborate for positive change: Think about the community issues that resonate with you. Reflect on how you can actively work together with others to solve these issues and create positive change. Consider joining local organizations, volunteering your time and skills, or initiating projects that address these challenges. Write down one specific action you can take to collaborate with others for positive change.

Embrace the journey: Remember that multiplying in purpose and impact is an ongoing process. It requires dedication, perseverance, and a commitment to personal growth. Embrace the journey and celebrate your progress along the way. Use this journal as a tool to track your development, reflect on challenges, and set new goals.

Seek inspiration from within and from those around you. By multiplying in quality, skill, and compassion, you can contribute to the betterment of your communities and make a positive impact on the world.

Card Reflection: Seed of Life

Shuffle your deck and lay out five cards side by side.

1. **The Seed:** What are your strengths and talents?
2. **The Growth:** Which skills do you need to develop or refine?
3. **The Compassion:** How can you cultivate empathy and love toward others?
4. **The Collaboration:** In what ways can you work together with others for positive change?
5. **The Potential:** What outcomes and possibilities await as you multiply in purpose and impact?

Affirmation

I co-create with the Universe.

CREATION OVER COMPETITION WITH THE DEVIL AND THE WORLD

In tarot readings, the Devil card represents the obstacles and temptations that hinder your goals, reminding you of your power to choose whether to give in or explore your shadows and embrace healing. The World card signifies fulfillment and success, achieved through taking an active role in shaping your life. When taken together, both cards emphasize your power to shape your destiny through your choices and actions.

In a world consumed by competition, consider shifting your perspective and embracing the power of creation. Life itself is a testament to your inherent drive to grow, expand, and replicate. Instead of getting caught up in the race to outdo others, explore the idea that your true purpose lies in creating and manifesting your desires. By tapping into your creative potential, you can unlock a world of abundance and fulfillment.

Every thought and talent you develop serves as a catalyst for further growth. You are a natural creator, with the ability to shape your own destiny. The Universe, in its infinite wisdom, wants you to have everything you need to live your best life. Recognize this innate drive within you and harness your creative power to build a life beyond your current limitations. True wealth is not measured by material possessions, but by your ability to fulfill your desires as they are in agreement with the greater good. Abundance exists everywhere, not just for a select few.

Remember, you are a creator. You are made to manifest your desires in life, as your desires represent your contribution to the greatest and highest good of all. So, next time when you fall into an us versus them or winner-loser mentality, consciously redirect that energy to imagining what you want to create. Align your thoughts to creation and your beliefs, habits, and actions will follow. And one day, you will wake up and see: you are living your purpose, and you have everything you need, always, inside of you. However, we still have to work and take the steps to align reality with desire.

Exercise: Embracing Creation Over Competition

In this exercise, you will delve into your competitive tendencies and explore how they may impact your ability to tap into your collaborative and creative spirit. Living in a more abundant and equal society begins with your ability to heal the spirit of extreme hierarchy within your body. By reflecting on moments of competition and shifting your focus toward collaboration, celebration of uniqueness, and setting meaningful goals, you can transform your mindset and unlock new realms of creativity and personal growth.

Take some time to ponder the following questions and record your thoughts in your journal.

When and how do you fall into us versus them thinking? How may sitting in this energy block your creativity?

Can you identify moments of competition and consider their impact on your growth?

Are you willing to shift your focus toward celebrating uniqueness instead of comparing yourself to others?

How can you foster collaboration and cooperation instead of engaging in rivalry?

What creative activities can you engage in without the need for comparison?

Have you set meaningful goals that prioritize personal growth over external validation?

Are you ready to transform your competitive spirit into a creative one, embracing collaboration and self-expression?

What new possibilities can open up for you when you embrace creation over competition?

Card Reflection: Create with Your Calling

Shuffle your deck and lay out seven cards side by side.

1. **Soul's Whisper:** What is your soul urging you to do?
2. **Motivation:** Why do you want it?
3. **Obstacles:** What is holding you back?
4. **Supportive Voices:** Who believes in you?
5. **Unsupportive Voices:** Who discourages you?
6. **Proactive Step:** Take a risk, what's the next move?
7. **Grounded Action:** What practical step can you take now?

Affirmation

The Universe has already equipped me with the necessary tools, resources, and relationships to bring my ideas into form.

WIN-WIN AS THE NEW GOLD STANDARD
WITH THE QUEEN OF PENTACLES

You are what you surround yourself with. When you act in agreement or synergy with the world around you, nature, and its ecology, you can create together. When you fail to live in synergy with the world—be it nature, its people, or its objects, both material and nonmaterial—you invite destruction.

The legal field has been marketed to the public as one of great conflict, tensions—a win-lose proposition. You see shows focusing on the drama between parties, who wins and who loses, and the rightness or not-rightness of a position. This legal drama plays out in other arenas as well, such as in sports, reality TV shows, political debates, and social justice movements. There is a prevalent mentality that if someone wins, the others must lose.

What is not shown, however, is that the 95 percent or more of legal transactions that do not go to trial focus on a win-win situation. Conflict is unavoidable in a diverse work where so many people are trying to create solutions for others. Especially in a fast-paced society, where there isn't the time to reflect on or perfectly communicate a position, misunderstandings occur, and legal battles escalate.

So, when faced with the choice, consider how to turn a win-lose into a win-win. When you focus on the win-win, you are able to give to others when they need to receive, and receive from others when they can give. It is this reciprocity that fuels creative ideas, businesses, ventures, partnerships, and other collaborations that heal our communities from both the inside out and the outside in.

Tarot Meditation: The New Gold Standard with the Queen of Pentacles

In this meditation, we will explore the energy of the Queen of Pentacles from the tarot deck, drawing inspiration from the principles of exceptional customer service outlined in *The New Gold Standard: 5 Leadership Principles for Creating a Legendary Customer Experience* by Joseph A. Michelli.

As you envision the Queen of Pentacles, see her as a symbol of nurturing and abundance. Just like a five-star hotel understands the importance of valuing their employees, imagine yourself embodying the qualities of a supportive and empowering leader. Visualize yourself creating a work environment that fosters happiness and engagement among your team members.

Now, focus on the art of anticipating the needs of others, just as the five-star hotel goes beyond meeting expectations. Picture yourself being perceptive and proactive in understanding the desires and preferences of those around you. Envision yourself providing personalized experiences that leave a lasting impact on others.

Feel the sense of empowerment within you. Like every employee at the five-star hotel, know that you have the power to take ownership of your interactions and resolve any issues that may arise. Embrace this empowerment, knowing that it not only boosts your own morale but also ensures that those you serve receive exceptional service.

Shift your attention to the importance of attention to detail, a hallmark of a five-star hotel. Imagine yourself paying close attention to every aspect of your work, from the smallest details to the grander picture. Envision yourself striving for perfection, just as the five-star hotel establishes an impression of luxury and excellence through their meticulous approach.

Finally, embrace the commitment to continuous improvement. Like the five-star hotel actively seek feedback from others to stay aligned with evolving expectations. Envision yourself listening attentively and implementing necessary changes to ensure that your service remains exceptional.

Take a deep breath and slowly open your eyes. Carry the energy of the Queen of Pentacles with you as you navigate your journey, bringing exceptional service and abundance to all you encounter.

Affirmation

I provide service to myself and the world in a way that demonstrates care, concern, and a commitment to reflection and redirection.

CAPRICORN III: CONSCIOUS RESOURCE MANAGEMENT

Four of Pentacles as Sun in Capricorn

Each decision we make today, each resource we carefully allocate, is a step toward creating a sustainable and prosperous future. This practice goes beyond mere financial gain; it reflects our values, our respect for what we have, and our vision for tomorrow. By managing resources consciously, we are not just building wealth, but also fostering a sense of responsibility and cultivating a mindset of abundance. You are the gardener of your life.

DEFINING AND REDEFINING SURPLUS

In today's fast-paced and consumer-driven world, it's important for you to define and understand the concept of surplus in relation to material resources. Surplus refers to an excess or abundance of resources beyond what you truly need for immediate necessities. Keep in mind that surplus is relative, meaning that what may be considered surplus to you might be an essential resource for someone else.

Defining terms such as surplus allows you to have a clear understanding of your possessions and their significance in your life. By defining surplus, you can accurately assess and evaluate your material resources, enabling you to make more mindful and informed choices when it comes to consumption.

Practicing resource accounting by taking stock of your belongings and evaluating their utility helps you gain a deeper understanding of what is truly essential to you. This process helps you avoid unnecessary waste and promotes responsible consumption.

Moreover, the analogy of reinvestment into the community being comparable to returning nutrients to the soil is a powerful one. When we have more than enough resources, hoarding them without reinvestment only leads to further disparities in society. Just as nutrients are essential for the growth and sustainability of the soil, reinvesting surplus resources back into the community is crucial for creating a more equitable society. By sharing our surplus, we contribute to the well-being of others and help alleviate unnecessary suffering.

Consider taking practical steps to avoid overconsumption, such as adopting an essentialist mindset, practicing conscious consumption, and fostering a culture of sharing. These steps empower you to make intentional decisions about what you consume and how you use your resources.

By clearly defining the terms surrounding surplus and material resources, you gain a better understanding of their relative nature and the importance of responsible consumption. It allows you to make more informed choices, reinvest your surplus into the community, and pave the way toward a more sustainable and equitable future.

Exercise: How Much Is Enough?

Reflect on your relationship with time and resources:

What recent actions have you taken to manage resources effectively? Recall instances where you consciously reduced waste, conserved energy, or used renewable resources.

How can you be more intentional with non-renewable resources like time? Identify areas where time is wasted or inefficiently utilized. Prioritize and organize your time for maximum impact. Have you joined local groups or organizations that are protecting natural resources? Consider your involvement in sustainability-focused initiatives. How can you contribute your skills and resources to support them?

How can you continue making a positive impact in your community? Ponder small changes promoting sustainability in your daily life. Support local farmers, reduce single-use plastics, or advocate for environmental policies. Inspire and engage others through your actions.

Approach these questions with persistence, resilience, and positivity. Remember, effectively managing resources is an ongoing journey toward a more sustainable world.

Affirmation

I give and receive in right proportion.

TIME IS YOUR MOST VALUABLE RESOURCE: SATURN AND SOLAR RETURNS

In our fast-paced world, time is a finite resource that we often undervalue. However, by understanding the concept of transaction costs and its relationship with time management, we can make more conscious decisions and maximize our productivity.

Transaction costs, in economic terms, refer to the expenses incurred when engaging in an exchange or transaction. These costs can include time, effort, resources, and even emotional energy. For example, imagine you need to buy groceries. You have two options: visiting a nearby store or ordering online. While the nearby store might offer convenience, it could involve the transaction cost of commuting and spending time physically shopping. On the other hand, online shopping might save time but could result in the transaction cost of delivery fees and potential delays.

Time management is about making intentional choices to prioritize and allocate our time effectively. To do this, it is crucial to consider transaction costs in relation to time. Time, being our most valuable resource, has transaction costs associated with various activities. The more time we spend on one task, the less time we have for other important activities.

When we fail to manage our time effectively, we encounter high transaction costs. Procrastination, disorganization, and lack of prioritization can all lead to wasted time and increased stress. On the other hand, effective time management minimizes transaction costs, allowing us to accomplish more in less time and reducing unnecessary effort.

Exercise: Calculating Transaction Costs

Take a few moments to reflect on your current use of time. Consider the following questions:

Which activities consume a significant amount of your time but provide little value or fulfillment?

How can you minimize transaction costs associated with time management in your daily life?

Are there any tasks or responsibilities that you could delegate or outsource to free up more time?

What steps can you take to better prioritize and plan your time?

How will effective time management positively impact your overall well-being and productivity?

Exercise: Saturn and Solar Returns

Astrological returns, such as Saturn and Solar returns, are important to living an astrologically-aligned life, and provide valuable insights into one's life journey. These returns occur when a planet returns to the exact degree and minute it occupied at the time of a birth chart event or a previous return. They provide a snapshot of the cosmic energies influencing a person's life during a specific timescale.

When it comes to Saturn returns, they occur approximately every 29.5 years, marking significant milestones in one's life. The first Saturn return, happening around the age of 29, signifies the transition from youth to adulthood, urging individuals to embrace responsibility and make important life decisions. The second Saturn return, taking place around the age of 58, brings a sense of reflection and potential restructuring, prompting individuals to evaluate past choices and seek fulfillment in their later years.

Solar returns, on the other hand, happen annually when the Sun returns to its natal position in an individual's birth chart. They offer valuable insights into the upcoming year, shedding light on various aspects of life such as career, relationships, and personal growth. By locating and analyzing the Solar return chart, astrologers can decipher the influence of planetary transits and their impact on different areas of life. For instance, the placement of Venus could indicate new romantic relationships or opportunities for creative expression, while challenging aspects may suggest potential obstacles or areas that require attention and growth.

Now, consider the following, and write down your responses in your journal:

What are your greatest strengths when it comes to managing time?

Weaknesses?

What monthly expenses go toward managing time?

How many hours do you dedicate to your job?

To your home life?

To your friends?

To your personal freedom?

Who in your support group can help you better manage time?

What actions can you take to improve your time management?

Affirmation

I live fully in the present moment in each moment because time is the only non-renewable resource that I have.

THE DECANS OF AQUARIUS

Dreams
Are the seeds
Of the New Earth

AQUARIUS I: A NEW EARTH

Five of Swords as Venus in Aquarius

In the heart of every human lies a seed—a potential Eden waiting to be nurtured, to bloom into existence. This seed is a symbol of our inherent connection to nature, an echo of a time when humanity and the earth were one harmonious entity. It is a call to return to Eden, not just as a physical place we are able to manifest on Planet Earth, but as a state of being, where love, hope, and harmony flourish like a vibrant, verdant garden.

RETURNING TO EDEN AS SEEDS

Much like seeds that carry within them the potential for new life, we too hold the power to replenish the Earth, sparking a renewal of vitality. As seeds, our role is to become nutrients for the soil of New Eden, effecting transformation in unprecedented ways. By tapping into our innate healing abilities, we can nurture our unique talents, stimulate growth in our local communities, and contribute to global healing.

In this symbolic garden of Eden, we realize that each one of us carries the latent energy of a seed. This seed represents the duality of our false self and true self. The false self is the outer shell, the persona we present to the world, often shaped by societal expectations and norms. The true self, however, lies within, waiting to germinate—it's our authentic self, our passions, and our unique skills. Just as seeds are vital for plant growth, acknowledging and nurturing our true self is crucial for our personal growth and the Earth's restoration.

Just as a seed sprouts from careful nurturing, we can start by recognizing and cultivating our true self, using it to foster growth in our local communities. Sharing our knowledge, honing our skills, and offering our resources contributes to collective progress. This could manifest in various forms like supporting local initiatives, volunteering, or leading projects that address societal and environmental challenges. As we care for our local communities, we plant seeds of change, promoting unity and well-being.

As we engage in this process of growth and community enrichment, we begin the work of healing the world. Each action that aligns with our true self becomes a seed of healing. Through acts of kindness, compassion, and sustainable practices, we create a positive impact on the environment and society. Much like gardens flourish with care, our collective efforts can cultivate a thriving Eden, where harmony and balance are restored.

In this journey of returning to Eden as seeds, we're not only healing the Earth but also nurturing our own spirits. Connecting with nature, recognizing our true self, and contributing to others' welfare leads to personal growth, satisfaction, and a deep sense of purpose. As we shed our false self and embrace our true self, the process of nurturing the world becomes reciprocal, as we find ourselves nurtured in return.

Each one of us has the power to be a seed of healing in both the metaphorical and actual garden of Eden that manifests here on Planet Earth. By recognizing our true self, cultivating our gifts, and using them to foster growth in our local communities, we play a vital role in Earth's restoration. Let's embrace our role as agents of positive change and strive to create a world that mirrors the harmony and abundance of the original Eden. Together, we can cultivate a garden of Eden that transcends geographical boundaries and cultural differences, healing the Earth and fostering a brighter future for all.

Card Reflection: A New Eden

Shuffle your deck and lay out three cards side by side. The first represents the seed (your potential), the second represents the soil (your local community), and the third represents New Eden (the impact of your actions on the world).

Affirmation

I am a seed of change, embodying my true self, carrying within me the potential for growth and healing. I nourish my community with my unique gifts, contributing to the restoration of the Earth.

BREAKING ORBIT WITH THE FIG LEAF

Isaac Newton's third law of motion states that for every action there is an equal and opposite reaction. So, when something is in orbit, it exists in equilibrium with the system surrounding it. In other words, it maintains the status quo. To break orbit (or the status quo), thrust is required. In this case, thrust means a force great enough to pierce and overcome the opposite force, if only for a moment, so that it can accelerate into the void of space until captured by the gravitational pull of another body or system.

When we seek freedom, what we are really seeking is the breaking of old habits and the trying on of new ways of being. We are seeking to break the gravitational pulls of toxic families, addictions, or relationships no longer suited to us. We look to break from old cultures, religious beliefs, and other constrictions that were once necessary for our lives and soul growth but are no longer needed.

Systemically, we look to break out of old patterns of collective thinking that are based on intentional exclusion (either express orimplied) of different races, religions, or cultures. When we break out of patterns of collective thinking, we codify these things into laws. This way, generations that come after us can remember the lessons learned from our generation and not repeat toxic cycles of war, poverty, and other destructive human behaviors. In many situations, we must start again from the beginning.

Breaking orbits and revising laws takes a lot of thrust. It is not easy. During the thrust stage, an individual or group may become so focused on their experience that they alienate others. They may seek to control others through denial and censorship. They may experience rage, anger, or frustration as they reorient themselves to move forward. The key during these moments is to allow our bodies to feel while also engaging our minds to allow emotions to pass through in a way that causes the least harm to others and nature.

When we break orbits, we say good-bye to our past selves. But remember that we don't need to destroy the past to move toward the future. For the past birthed us, and it gave us all we need to create our new desires.

Exercise: Working with the Fig to Learn How to Create in a New World

The fig leaf, with its rich symbolism and cultural significance, serves as a powerful metaphor for personal growth and self-creation. When we embrace the fig leaf as a symbol of readiness, we signify our preparedness to embark on a transformative journey to discover our own power of creation.

Traditionally, the fig tree represents our earthly nature as co-creators, reminding us of our innate ability to shape our lives and manifest our desires. Like the fig tree, we have the potential to bear fruit, to bring forth new creations and experiences. By embracing this symbolism, we recognize that we are not passive recipients of life's circumstances but active participants in the process of creation.

Furthermore, the fig's resemblance to a woman's womb signifies a fertile time in our lives—a period ripe with possibilities and opportunities for growth. Just as the fig tree produces an abundance of seeds, we too can tap into our creative energy and desires, nurturing them with intention and purpose.

Rather than relying on others to create for us, the fig leaf symbolizes the duplication of power. It calls us to take responsibility for our own creations and to return any excess to the divine, recognizing our interconnectedness with the Universe. We shift from being mere recipients of creation to active contributors, becoming an integral part of the creative process itself.

Throughout history, the fig tree has been associated with wisdom, abundance, and the sacred. In ancient Egypt, it represented the primordial earth mothers and the Tree of Life. In the Bible, it is mentioned alongside the Tree of Life and the Tree of Knowledge, highlighting its significance in human spirituality and self-discovery. The fig is then referenced in the book of Revelation with the "stars in the sky fell to the earth, as figs drop from a fig tree when shaken by a strong wind" and could be one of the 12 fruits produced by the Tree of Life for the healing of the nations in the last chapter of Revelation.

By embracing the symbol of the fig leaf, we open ourselves to the limitless possibilities of self-creation. We tap into our collective memory of belonging to each other and share our creative energy with the world. Just as the fig tree inspires the sharing of its fruits, we too can share our unique gifts and talents with others, fostering a sense of interconnectedness and unity.

In conclusion, the fig leaf serves as a powerful symbol of readiness to embark on a journey of self-creation. It reminds us that we have the power to shape our lives, manifest our desires, and contribute to the creative tapestry of existence. By embracing this symbolism, we step into our own power and become active participants in the process of creation.

Card Reflection: Reaching Escape Velocity

Shuffle your deck and lay out five cards side by side.

1. **Current Orbit:** What patterns or habits are currently keeping you in an orbit that you don't want to be in?

2. **The Thrust:** What one action or force is needed for you to break free?

3. **The Void:** What challenges or feelings do you encounter?

4. **New Orbit:** What new patterns, habits, or systems will you need to create to enter a new orbit?

5. **Resources:** What resources or support do you require?

Affirmation

I embrace the wisdom and abundance that comes from tapping into my creative power, knowing that I am an active participant in the process of creation.

AQUARIUS II: TRANSPOSING EARTH TO A NEW KEY

Six of Swords as Mercury in Aquarius
Our first language is music.

ASTROLOGY AS THE CONCERT PITCH

There was a time when every town had its own unique sound, tuned to the local organ. Over time, as orchestras grew and music became more complex, the need for standardization emerged.

The concept of concert pitch has since evolved, with the tuning fork playing a critical role in its standardization. In 1953, the International Standards Organization declared A440 Hz as the universal concert pitch, setting a standard for musical harmony worldwide.

However, just like the currents of a river, the pitch has been subtly shifting. Continental Europe has seen a rise in pitch to A442 or even A444, while the UK and USA have largely adhered to A440. This continuous evolution of pitch symbolizes our dynamic world, reflecting our capacity to adapt and innovate.

This journey of concert pitch offers a compelling analogy for the transformations needed in our world today. As we face global challenges such as climate change and pandemics, we must learn to tune our actions and attitudes toward a collective purpose, much like an orchestra tunes its diverse instruments to the same note.

An orchestra is a beautiful ensemble of diverse instruments, each with its unique sound but all working together to create harmonious music. Similarly, our world thrives on diversity, with each individual contributing to the collective symphony of life. However, to address the global issues we face, we must find our common note—our shared goals and objectives that resonate with all.

In the vast tapestry of human existence, individual cultural practices, religions, and spiritual traditions each possess their own unique melodies. Like distinct instruments in an orchestra, these diverse expressions of faith and belief bring forth a rich array of strengths, tones, and qualities. And when they come together, they harmonize to create a symphony of creation.

Just as different cultures have developed their own musical traditions, astrology serves as a universal language that weaves through these diverse practices. It recognizes that while each tradition may have its own rhythms and harmonies, they all share a common thread—the aspiration to understand and connect with the cosmic forces that shape our lives.

Astrology embraces the beauty of these individual traditions, honoring their wisdom and deep-rooted cultural significance. It acknowledges that each practice carries a unique perspective on the cosmic dance, adding depth and richness to the collective symphony of human experience.

When we open ourselves to the symphony of diverse cultural practices and spiritual traditions, we discover that they are not meant to be played in isolation. Instead, they are truly brought to life when they intertwine, creating a harmonious blend that transcends individual boundaries.

Just as an orchestra conductor brings together musicians from various backgrounds, astrology encourages us to explore and appreciate the multifaceted nature of spirituality. It invites us to listen to the melodies of different cultures, religions, and spiritual practices, recognizing the value they bring to the grand orchestration of life.

By embracing this diversity, we discover that the symphony of creation is enriched by the unique contributions of each individual cultural practice and spiritual tradition. They become the building blocks of a harmonious and inclusive society where the strengths of one complement the strengths of another.

In this symphony of collaboration, we find unity amidst diversity. Each instrument—each cultural practice and spiritual tradition—finds its place in the grand composition of existence. Together, they create a chorus that celebrates the multifaceted nature of humanity and the interconnectedness of our collective journey.

As we immerse ourselves in the symphony of cultural practices and spiritual traditions, we come to appreciate the intricate interplay of harmonies and melodies. We recognize that it is through the convergence of these diverse expressions that we can truly understand the vastness of the cosmic symphony.

Astrology as the concert pitch invites us to embrace and celebrate the beauty of our differences. It teaches us to honor and learn from one another, recognizing that the symphony of creation is most vibrant when we blend our unique tones into a harmonious whole.

Astrology serves as a guiding light that encourages us to appreciate and unite the strengths, tones, and qualities of each individual cultural practice, religion, and spiritual tradition. By embracing the symphony of diversity, we create a world where all voices are heard, and the universal harmony of existence resounds with a clarity and beauty that transcends boundaries.

Exercise: What Frequency Are You Tuned To?

Reflect on what pitch, so to speak, you are currently tuned to in your life. Are there areas where you need to adjust your pitch to align better with your personal goals, with the goals of your local community, your state government, your federal government, or the larger goals of humanity? Write about what steps you can take to make these adjustments.

Card Reflection: Getting in Tune with the Collective

Draw three cards. The first represents the current pitch or frequency of your life. The second symbolizes the pitch you aspire to reach. The third provides guidance on how to bridge the gap between the two.

Affirmation

I respect and honor the interconnectedness of all life, understanding that my choices impact the global symphony.

RAISING THE CONSCIOUSNESS OF THE WORLD WITH SATURN

Elevating the planet's vibration requires more than just positive emotions; it necessitates acknowledging the full spectrum of human experience, including those aspects we might not favor. These facets serve as crucial data, guiding us toward areas within ourselves that need transformation. This concept is reminiscent of James Lovelock's Gaia hypothesis, which perceives Earth as a living organism with self-regulating mechanisms.

It is here that the Saturn archetype enters the scene. Symbolizing discipline, responsibility, and limitation, Saturn invites us to draw boundaries on ourselves before Mother Earth imposes them upon us. It's about assuming responsibility for our actions and respecting the boundaries of our existence, enabling us to coexist harmoniously with nature rather than clash against it.

Raising global consciousness isn't merely about nurturing good vibes. It involves translating these vibes into healed bodies capable of transforming societies. Just as plants adapt to their local ecology, humans too are designed with nuances specific to their regions. When we detach ourselves from these environments, we risk depleting local resources and wisdom.

In the plant world, weeds often come up in areas where the soil is too dry or otherwise lacking in a much-needed nutrient. Likewise, we encounter societal "weeds" or individuals expressing views that we find challenging to comprehend or accept. Dismissing them could mean overlooking key data about our community's health. Empathy and a readiness to learn from diverse perspectives are vital for community healing. By fostering awareness, cultivating intimate relationships with our bodies, and achieving a healed state within ourselves, we can contribute to global healing.

Sound healing, acoustics, and personal growth are formidable tools for both personal and planetary transformation. By aligning our inner rhythms with the cosmos and embracing the lessons of the Saturn archetype, we can pave the way for a more conscious and compassionate world.

Exercise: A Seven-Day Sound Healing Journey

Day 1: Tuning in to Your Frequency

Reflect on the concept that every entity in the Universe vibrates at a unique frequency, including you. How does this make you feel? Do you feel connected to the greater universal orchestra? Write down your thoughts and feelings about this principle.

Day 2: Exploring Sound Therapies

Research different types of sound therapies that resonate with you. It could be anything from Tibetan singing bowls to binaural beats. Write down why these particular therapies appeal to you and how you think they might help enhance your wellness.

Day 3: Creating Your Healing Space

Evaluate your living or working space in terms of its acoustics. Is it conducive for sound healing? If not, what changes can you make? Make a list of adjustments you could apply to create an environment more receptive to sound healing.

Day 4: Experimenting with Sound Healing Tools

Choose one sound healing tool or technique that you researched on Day 2. Spend some time experimenting with it. This could involve listening to binaural beats before bed or trying out vocal toning. Write down your experience and any changes you notice in your stress levels, sleep quality, or overall wellness.

Day 5: Aligning with Your Energy Fields

Reflect on the idea of aligning your body's energy fields through precise frequencies, much like a tuning fork adjusts an instrument. How do you feel about this concept? Do you believe it's possible to recalibrate your balance using sound? Write down your thoughts.

Day 6: Tapping into Your Healing Power

Experiment with using your own voice as a tool for healing. Try vocal toning and note how different tones resonate with various parts of your body. Write about your experience and any sensations or emotions that arose during the process.

Day 7: Reflecting on Your Sound Healing Journey

Reflect on your journey over the past week. Have you noticed any changes in your well-being? Do you feel more in tune with the Universe's grand orchestra? Write down your observations, insights, and how you plan to incorporate sound healing into your regular wellness routine.

Card Reflection: Moving from Healing to Transformation with Sound

Shuffle your deck and lay out three cards side by side.

1. **Your Personal Symphony:** This card represents your individual vibration within the universal orchestra and the form of sound therapy that resonates with you at this moment. It provides insights into your current energy state and suggests a healing method that might be beneficial for you.

2. **Your Healing Journey:** This card reveals the energy of your current environment, how well you're aligning with your energy fields, and the specific sound healing tool or technique that could aid you. It offers guidance on how your space supports or hinders your sound healing journey and where adjustments might be needed.

3. **Your Transformation:** This card represents your
    potential to heal yourself through sound and voice,
    reflecting the transformation you've undergone
    during your sound healing journey. It suggests
    the path forward, encouraging self-reflection and
    personal growth.

Affirmation

I am attuned to the symphony of sounds that interact with my
energy field, fostering a rhythmic sense of balance and harmony
within me.

PSYCHEDELICS OPTIONAL WITH THE KING OF SWORDS

In his deeply personal memoir, *Fishers of Men*, Adam Elenbaas
portrays his spiritual journey from religious disillusionment to
profound awakening. His path was facilitated using ayahuasca, a
potent psychedelic native to the Amazon rainforest. However, it's
crucial to note that while Elenbaas's spiritual evolution was significantly influenced by psychedelics, these substances are not the
sole gateways to spiritual experiences or divine understanding.

Spirituality is a highly individual journey, and psychedelics
may serve as a catalyst for self-discovery for some. Yet, these substances are not essential or recommended for everyone. A classical education, rooted in the humanities and sciences, can also
lead to spiritual enlightenment. By studying philosophy, literature, history, and the natural world, one can develop a profound
appreciation for life's complexity and interconnectedness. This
understanding can cultivate a sense of awe and reverence typically associated with spirituality.

Spiritual experiences often evoke feelings of transcendence,
unity, and a connection with something greater than oneself. These

experiences can be instigated through various non-psychedelic means, such as meditation, prayer, nature immersion, or engaging in meaningful work or service.

In the same vein, understanding the physiology of the nervous system can support your spiritual growth if you dedicate yourself to studying how these structures cooperate to transmit signals throughout the body. A key element of comprehending the nervous system is learning how to regulate it. Practices that aid in becoming more acutely aware of, feeling into, and mindfully regulating the body's response to stress, including deep breathing exercises, meditation, and other mindfulness techniques, are essential in this regard.

Notably, clinical psychologist Dr. Nicole LePera has made substantial contributions to understanding the role of the vagus nerve in emotional trauma healing. The vagus nerve, part of the parasympathetic nervous system, plays a crucial role in regulating the body's stress response. According to Dr. LePera, stimulating the vagus nerve through practices like deep breathing and meditation can facilitate this regulation and promote healing.

The journey to spiritual growth can be multifaceted. A classical education, combined with an understanding of our own physiology and practices like meditation, and a coach or community to provide accountability and support, can also guide individuals toward profound spiritual experiences and a deeper understanding of God.

Tarot Meditation: Developing the Whole-Mind with the King of Swords

Begin by visualizing the King of Swords. Picture him in all his majesty, symbolizing intellectual power, clarity of thought, truth, and fairness. He stands as a beacon of critical thinking and clear communication, qualities nurtured by classical liberal arts training.

As you visualize the King of Swords, consider each of the seven liberal arts—Grammar, Logic, Rhetoric, Arithmetic, Geometry, Music, and Astronomy. Each of these subjects provides a unique lens through which to view and understand the world around us. They foster intellectual versatility, ethical judgment, and a life-long love of learning.

Now, imagine yourself holding the sword of the King, representing your well-rounded knowledge and understanding honed through rigorous thought and inquiry. Feel its weight, its balance, its potential. This is your tool to cut through confusion and illusion, to navigate complexities with refined intellect and clear communication.

As you hold this symbolic sword, reflect on where in your life you need to embody the qualities of the King of Swords. Where can you improve upon one of the seven liberal arts? Your grammar knowledge and application? Your training in logic? In rhetoric? In arithmetic? Geometry? Music? Astronomy? Each of these seven disciplines helps train the mind in different ways making the critical mind strong yet flexible.

Take your time with these reflections. There's no rush. Allow the insights to arise naturally, guided by the wisdom of the King of Swords and the power of the classical liberal arts.

Remember, while some choose to explore psychedelics in their journey of self-discovery, it is not the only path. The combination of classical liberal arts training and mindful meditation offers a potent catalyst for introspection and enlightenment.

As you conclude your meditation, gradually bring your awareness back to the present moment. Open your eyes, take a deep breath, and carry the wisdom of the King of Swords with you. Trust in your intellectual strength and your ability to discern truth from illusion. You have the power to navigate your life with confidence, clarity, and wisdom.

Affirmation

I embody intellectual power and the ability to hold multiple perspectives at once. I choose my next steps from a place of personal sovereignty and authority.

AQUARIUS III: RELEASING ENERGETIC BLOCKS IN THE NERVOUS SYSTEM

Seven of Swords as Moon in Aquarius
Our bodies know the way.

WE ARE THE SALT OF THE EARTH

"We are the salt of the earth" is a phrase that holds a profound truth about our existence. Just like the grains of salt, each of us is unique, essential, and capable of making a significant difference in the world. But just as too much salt can tip the balance and affect the flavor of a dish, an excess or lack of salt in our bodies can disrupt our well-being.

The sodium-potassium pump, a microscopic engine within your nerve cells, maintains a delicate balance of particles crucial to your nervous system's functioning. This pump moves three sodium ions out and two potassium ions into the cell, creating an electrical imbalance. When a stimulus occurs, such as touching a hot surface, this imbalance changes, triggering a rapid signal from your hand to your brain. This process highlights the importance of maintaining a balanced salt intake for optimum nerve function.

Our bodies' intricate salt-regulating systems have not changed significantly since the dawn of life. We retain salt when it's scarce and excrete it when it's abundant. This ability has allowed us to survive and thrive in different geographical regions. Yet, our blood still mirrors the ancient ocean where life began, tightly regulated to meet our species' specific requirements.

But what happens when this balance is off? The effects can be compared to melting freshwater ice into the sea, disrupting the ocean's salt balance. This shift can alter ocean currents and weather patterns, making certain parts of the world more habitable and others less so. Similarly, an imbalance in our body's salt levels can lead to health issues like hypertension, stroke, and cardiovascular disease, affecting our overall well-being and energy levels.

So, how can we ensure we maintain a healthy equilibrium? The key lies in self-awareness and monitoring. Start by tracking your sodium intake. There are tools available online that can help you keep tabs on your diet's sodium content. Experiment with different foods and salt balances. Pay attention to how your body reacts. Does a particular diet give you more energy or make you feel lethargic? Remember, the best person to understand your body is you.

Just as our ancestors adapted their diets to their environments, we can also adjust our salt intake based on our individual needs and inherited tendencies. By taking control of our health, we can prevent burnout, feel more energized, and live more fulfilling lives.

We are indeed the salt of the earth. By maintaining our body's salt balance, we not only secure our health but also contribute to the world's well-being. So let's embrace our uniqueness, monitor our salt intake, and remember—we have the power to make a difference, one grain of salt at a time.

Exercise: Salt Equilibrium Self-Reflection

Begin with pondering the concept of equilibrium. What does it mean to you? It could be a state of physical balance, a calm mind, or perhaps a harmonious lifestyle. Your personal definition of equilibrium will shape the course of this journey, so take a moment to write down your thoughts.

Next, turn your attention to your current diet. Consider the amount of salt you consume daily. Does it feel like too much, or could it be too little? It's important to remember that salt isn't inherently bad—it's about maintaining the right flow. Pay attention to how your body responds to your current salt intake. Do you notice any impact on your mood and energy levels? Your body often communicates what it needs; we just need to listen carefully.

Now, consider practical ways you can monitor your sodium intake. Perhaps you could start reading food labels more attentively, use a food- tracking app, or consult a professional. List down three methods that suit your lifestyle the best. Remember, the aim here is not to create a restrictive regime but to develop a greater awareness of your dietary habits.

Moving forward, brainstorm ways to shift your diet to agree with your desired energy levels. One way is to recall a time when you felt physically balanced and recall a time when you felt physically imbalanced. Consider diet, environment, emotions, and life circumstances. Reflect on the circumstances that led to this state and more importantly, how you restored your flow.

Remember, this journey toward finding your equilibrium is deeply personal. It's about developing an intimate understanding of your body's needs and responding with care and kindness.

Affirmation

I trust in my body's wisdom, knowing it communicates its needs through subtle signals.

HEALING WITH RUBATO AND URANUS

Rubato is a musical term that refers to the flexible tempo that allows musicians to inject emotion and depth into their performances by subtly accelerating or decelerating the pace. When we discuss healing and the body, rubato symbolizes our capacity to modify and adapt our rhythms to restore equilibrium and encourage healing.

The human body, akin to a musical composition, needs harmony and balance to function at its best. As a musician employs rubato to add richness and complexity to a piece, so can we apply the principles of rubato—flexibility, adaptation, and personal expression—to steer our path toward recovery.

The Alexander Technique is an approach designed to change movement habits in our daily routines. It's a straightforward and practical method for enhancing ease and freedom of movement, balance, support, and coordination. The technique promotes the use of the appropriate amount of effort for a specific activity, thus providing more energy for all your tasks.

In the Alexander Technique, the concept of rubato comes into play as the idea of flexibility and adaptation in our body movements and postures. This method encourages us to tune in to our bodies, to decelerate or accelerate as needed, essentially "borrowing" time and energy from areas where we have excess and investing it in areas that require it more.

For instance, one might learn to borrow effort from the habitual tightening of the neck and invest it into maintaining a balanced head-spine relationship, an essential principle in the Alexander Technique. This shift can lead to improved posture, reduced muscular tension, and even alleviation of chronic pain.

In the end, the journey toward healing begins with listening to our bodies. Our bodies possess an inherent wisdom and capacity for healing, much like how a musical piece holds the potential for a moving performance. By applying the principles of rubato and the Alexander Technique, we can tap into this potential, adjusting and adapting our bodily rhythms to promote balance, ease, and healing.

Exercise: Dialogue with Your Body

This exercise will help you tune into your body's signals, understand its language of aches and pains, and identify the support it needs to regain optimal health.

Find a quiet space and take a few deep breaths. Close your eyes and scan your body from head to toe. Notice any tension, discomfort, or pain? Open your journal and write down what you observed. Where is the pain located? What does it feel like? Is it constant or does it come and go? Now, imagine your body can speak. What might it be trying to tell you through these sensations? What does it need to heal? Write this down as well. Reflect on your entries. Are there patterns you notice? Are there actionable steps you can take, like adjusting your posture, taking breaks, or seeking professional help? Repeat this exercise daily for at least two weeks. Over time, you'll start understanding your body more and become better equipped to provide it with the care it needs.

Affirmation

I honor my body and its wisdom.

THE DECANS OF PISCES

And the first seed
Became a rose.

PISCES I: RETURNING TO THE HEART

Eight of Cups as Saturn in Pisces

We live in a world that often distracts us from our true selves, pulling us away from the essence of who we are. But here's the truth: the path to personal healing begins when we return to our heart center, our home. Just like a tree finds its strength in its roots, we too find our power when we reconnect with our inner selves. Imagine a river flowing steadily, finding its way back to the ocean where it belongs. In the same way, when we come back to our heart center, we reclaim our authenticity, our passion, and our purpose. It is in this place of alignment that we can tap into our innate wisdom and embrace the journey of healing. So today, let us reflect on our own journeys, remember our roots, and find our way back home, for it is there that we find ourselves and our healing is complete.

PISCES, THE HEALER

Pisces, as an archetype, is deeply associated with healing and spirituality. People who identify as Piscean possess innate qualities that enable them to tap into the realms of compassion and empathy, making them natural healers in both physical and spiritual senses. It is interesting to note that Jesus Christ himself, revered by many as a divine healer, was believed by some astrologers to be a Pisces.

The characteristics of Pisces revolve around their deep sensitivity and understanding of the emotions of others. They have an uncanny ability to connect with the pain and suffering of those around them, offering solace and support. This innate compassion allows them to act as conduits for healing energy, whether through emotional support, spiritual guidance, or even the creative arts. Pisceans are often drawn to fields such as counseling, therapy, spirituality, or any profession that involves helping others navigate their emotional depths.

In mythology and iconography, fish play a significant role in Piscean symbolism. The fish, representing duality and fluidity, mirror the nature of Pisces. As water signs, Pisceans are known for their adaptability and intuition, effortlessly flowing between different emotional states. The image of two fish swimming in opposite directions also symbolizes the constant struggle between reality and the dream world that Pisceans often find themselves navigating. This dualistic nature further connects them to the realm of healing, as they offer a bridge between the conscious and subconscious realms.

The Pisces archetype encompasses a profound sense of spirituality, healing, and compassion. Those born under this sign possess a unique ability to tap into the depths of human emotion, offering understanding, comfort, and guidance. Their intuitive nature and connection to higher realms make them natural conduits for healing energy. Whether it be through empathic interactions, spiritual practices, or creative endeavors, Pisceans embody the essence of the healer, bringing solace and transformation to those around them.

Exercise: Earth Water Ritual

Baptism is a symbolic act of purification and initiation often associated with water. It represents a conscious choice of transformation and renewal, an entry into a spiritual journey. While traditionally linked to Christianity, the essence of baptism—a form of rebirth or transition—transcends specific religious boundaries. It can be seen as an individual's commitment to a path of spiritual growth, irrespective of the tradition they choose to follow. The act of submerging oneself in water can have a deeply calming effect on the nervous system.

In an increasingly diverse and fragmented world, water rituals can play a pivotal role in fostering a sense of community and unity. As we gather around riversides, lakes, or even communal baths, we honor and respect a shared resource. These practices transcend cultural, religious, and social boundaries, reminding us of our shared humanity and our collective responsibility toward nature.

Participating in these rituals also encourages a more mindful approach to life and our environment. They make us pause, reflect, and appreciate the fundamental role water plays in our existence. In an age characterized by overconsumption and environmental degradation, these moments of reflection are not just spiritually enriching; they are vital for our planet's survival.

So, how can we incorporate this appreciation for water into our daily lives? It could be as simple as mindful consumption, being aware of the water we use and waste. Or it could be participating in local water rituals or creating our own, using these moments to connect with our community, nature, and ourselves.

Water rituals offer us a path to return to our roots, to reconnect with our environment, and to remind ourselves of the delicate balance that sustains life on Earth. As we navigate the challenges of the 21st century, let's draw from the wisdom of the past and embrace these water rituals as a beacon of unity, mindfulness, and environmental stewardship.

Affirmation

I honor and respect water as a source of life, renewal, and unity. With mindfulness, I contribute to its preservation and foster a stronger bond with nature and my community.

THE POWER OF A QUESTION

In the biblical narrative of the book of Revelation, we find powerful connections between the act of questioning and the potential for profound transformation. Here, questioning plays a crucial role in individual exploration and discovery. The apostle John, exiled on the island of Patmos, receives visions and revelations that challenge conventional wisdom and invite introspection. Throughout the book, John repeatedly asks questions, seeking deeper understanding and unraveling layers of meaning.

The power of questioning lies in its ability to disrupt complacency, provoke critical thinking, and inspire personal growth. By questioning the established order, individuals can challenge assumptions, examine their own beliefs and values, and embark on a journey of self-discovery. It is through questioning that we gain insight, expand our perspectives, and find the courage to forge our own paths.

In a world driven by certainty and conformity, the act of questioning stands as a beacon of intellectual and spiritual liberation. As we embrace our innate curiosity and dare to question, we step into a realm of infinite possibilities, where our beliefs, values, and convictions are refined, strengthened, and made wholly our own.

Exercise: Curiosity Didn't Kill the Cat

Cats can be seen as creatures of mystery and curiosity, their independent spirits and unpredictable behavior symbolizing the enigmatic mysteries of life itself. You can use this cat energy to help process the gray areas of life, employing the steps of the scientific method–observation, hypothesis, experiment, results, and conclusion.

Step 1: Feline Observation

Identify an area in your life that's as elusive as a mouse darting in the shadows. With the keen eye of a lioness on the hunt, observe all the details of this situation. Write down everything you notice. What patterns do you see? How does it make you feel?

Step 2: Crafting Hypotheses with Catlike Precision

Like a cheetah calculating its sprint, formulate a hypothesis about what changes could improve this situation. A hypothesis is a calculated guess that you can test through experiments. If your job leaves you feeling as empty as a food bowl at the end of the day, your hypothesis might be: "If I dedicate one hour each day to learning new skills, I will find more satisfaction in my work."

Step 3: Experiment with the Agility of a Jaguar

With the agility and adaptability of a jaguar, design an experiment to test your hypothesis. This could involve setting aside one hour each day to learn new skills related to your job. Ensure your experiment is achievable and write down your plan of action.

Step 4: Tracking Results like a Hunting Lioness

As you carry out your experiment, track your results with the precision of a lioness tracking her prey. How does each learning session make you feel? Do you notice any changes in your attitude toward your job? Remember, patience is key—transformation takes time, just like a successful hunt.

Step 5: Concluding Like a Satisfied Housecat

After a set period (perhaps as long as a cat's leisurely nap), review your notes and draw a conclusion. Has your job satisfaction improved? If not, don't worry. Just as a cat is persistent in its pursuits, you can always refine your hypothesis and experiment again.

By embracing the energy of a cat in your personal transformation journey, you can navigate the gray areas of life with curiosity, precision, and resilience. Remember, the goal isn't to catch every mouse but to gain insights that can guide your growth. Keep observing, hypothesizing, experimenting, tracking, and concluding.

Affirmation

I trust my intuition to guide me toward meaningful conclusions and have the courage to apply new insights and test their impact on my life.

THE HIGH PRIESTESS BRINGS SKY WATER TO COMPLETE OUR HEALING

Water is a universal symbol of life, renewal, and transformation. In many cultures and spiritual traditions, it is seen as a sacred element, connecting us to the divine and to each other. The water of the sky and the water of the earth, though seemingly different, are in fact part of the same cycle, reflecting the interconnectedness of all life.

The water of the sky represents the ethereal, the divine, and the intangible aspects of existence. It encompasses the rains that fall from the heavens, the dew that adorns the morning grass, and the clouds that dance across the skies. This water symbolizes our emotions, our dreams, and our spiritual journeys. It invites us to look up, to dream big, and to connect with the divine.

On the other hand, the water of the earth is tangible, grounding, and nurturing. It includes the rivers that carve their path through the landscape, the oceans that cradle an abundance of life, and the wellsprings that quench our thirst. This water symbolizes our physical existence, our everyday realities, and our connection to Mother Earth.

While we often perceive these realms as separate, they are, in fact, deeply intertwined. The water that falls from the sky nourishes the earth, allowing life to flourish. Similarly, the water from the earth evaporates, ascending to the sky, only to return as rain. This cycle reminds us that our physical and spiritual journeys are interconnected, that our actions have consequences, and that we are a part of something much larger than ourselves.

The High Priestess embodies this potent symbolism of water. She encourages us to honor both the water of the sky (our intuition, emotions, and spiritual journey) and the water of the earth (our physical existence, daily realities, and connection to nature). She also reminds us of the importance of staying true to our path.

So, whether you find peace in the sanctifying waters of a bapitsmal ritual, the steady pulse of ocean waves, the serene stream of a river, or even in the mystical dance of clouds forming in the sky, offering signs for divination, or the rain cascading down during a thunderstorm—always remember, water is a powerful emblem of life, rebirth, and metamorphosis. By respecting and honoring this sacred element, we can nurture our spiritual growth, contribute to the collective good, and help consciously care for our planet the way she cares for us.

Exercise: Pomegranates from the Tree of Life

When embarking on a new project or undertaking a significant life change, ritualizing the process can provide a meaningful and symbolic way to honor new beginnings. Drawing upon the imagery of the Tree of Life, the High Priestess, and the pomegranate fruit as powerful symbols, we can create a ritual that encompasses growth, intuition, and fertility.

To begin, set up a sacred space for your ritual. Place a representation of the Tree of Life, such as a beautifully crafted pendant or artwork, at the center. The Tree of Life symbolizes the interconnectedness of all aspects of life and serves as a reminder of growth and prosperity. Light candles around the tree, one for each branch, as a representation of the divine energy flowing through each aspect of your new venture.

Next, incorporate the High Priestess into the ritual. This card embodies female intuition, wisdom, and deep introspection. Meditate on its imagery, allowing it to inspire and guide you in making important decisions during this new phase. Consider pulling the card from a tarot deck and reflect on its message, trusting your inner voice as you navigate this transition.

Lastly, incorporate the significance of the pomegranate fruit. Cut open a ripe pomegranate, symbolizing fertility, abundance, and new life. As you consume the juicy seeds, visualize yourself nourishing your dreams and aspirations, infusing them with vitality and growth. You may also sprinkle some pomegranate seeds on the ground, symbolizing the seeds of potential that you are sowing in this new endeavor.

Throughout the ritual, take time to reflect on the symbolism of each element and how it relates to your personal journey. Embrace the energy of growth, tapping into your intuition to make empowered decisions, and celebrate the abundance of new opportunities.

The Healing Power of the Sky Water Tarot Card Spread

The High Priestess card serves as a potent symbol for this tarot spread, reminding us of the transformative power of water. Just as the water cycle nourishes the earth, bringing life and growth, so too can we draw upon the healing power of rain to foster personal growth and transformation.

Card 1 — The Rainfall: What emotions are currently pouring into your life? This card symbolizes the cleansing power of rain, washing away what no longer serves you and making room for new growth.

Card 2 — The Flow: Where is the current of your life leading you? This card represents the river's journey, moving toward its destination with purpose and momentum.

Card 3 — The Still Waters: What hidden depths do you need to explore within yourself? Like the tranquil surface of a lake, this card invites introspection and self-discovery.

Card 4 — The Evaporation: What aspects of your life are ready to transform and ascend? As water evaporates, it leaves behind its old form, signifying change and evolution.

Card 5 — The Clouds: What dreams or aspirations are gathering force in your life? Clouds are the promise of future rainfall, symbolizing potential and anticipation.

Card 6 — The Storm: What challenges are stirring on your horizon? Storms can be tumultuous but also bring much-needed change and refreshment.

Card 7 — The Rainbow: What hope or promise lies ahead after the storm? The rainbow is a symbol of hope, renewal, and the rewards that come after enduring difficulties.

As you draw each card, contemplate its symbolism in relation to the corresponding stage of the water cycle. Reflect on the ebb and flow of your own life, the transformative power of your emotions, and the infinite possibilities that lie within you, just as countless seeds lie within a pomegranate. Remember, every part of the cycle, from the calmest lake to the most tempestuous storm, has its purpose and its power. Embrace the healing power of rain and the wisdom of the High Priestess and let them guide you on your journey of self-discovery.

Affirmation

As I heal myself, I contribute to the healing of the world, creating a ripple effect of positive transformation.

PISCES II: RECONCILING INDIVIDUAL DESIRE WITH COLLECTIVE NEED

Nine of Cups as Jupiter in Pisces
We are all connected.

THE PRAYER NETWORK

Yoga, with its roots in ancient Indian philosophy, is more than a physical exercise. It's a holistic practice that integrates mind, body, and spirit, fostering inner peace, mindfulness, and a balanced life. The practice of yoga can contribute to reducing stress, enhancing mental clarity, improving physical health, and promoting spiritual growth.

Some studies suggest that collective practices like yoga and meditation can have a measurable impact on societal harmony. Prayer, much like yoga, also has the power to influence collective consciousness. When we pray, we tap into a universal energy field, connecting with others on a deep, spiritual level. This act of connection can foster a sense of unity, empathy, and understanding, helping us to navigate our shared experiences with compassion and grace.

Moreover, prayer can serve as a form of collective healing. As we send out positive intentions and seek divine guidance, we contribute to a healing energy that permeates our communities, our societies, and our world. In this way, individual prayers can ripple outwards, impacting the collective consciousness in profound and meaningful ways.

By embracing transformative practices like yoga and prayer, we not only nurture our own well-being but also contribute to a more harmonious and peaceful world. We hold significant power to create positive change, both within ourselves and in our collective consciousness.

Exercise: Working with Mary, Star of the Sea

Mary, Star of the Sea, has been a beacon of hope and guidance for centuries. This ancient title for the Blessed Virgin Mary was first used in the 9th century, translated from the Latin "Stella Maris." The name is believed to have originated from a misinterpretation of her Hebrew name, Miryam, meaning "drop of the sea."

As a star guiding sailors through tumultuous seas, Mary represents a spiritual navigator, helping us reconcile our individual desires with the needs of the collective. In times of personal turmoil or societal upheaval, turning to Mary, Star of the Sea, can provide solace and direction.

In the realm of self-help, prayer, or intentional communication with the divine, serves as a powerful tool for connection. When we pray, we connect not only with a higher power but also with the collective consciousness of humanity. This practice allows us to tap into universal wisdom, aligning our personal journey with the greater good.

Tarot cards can be a valuable tool in this process. They serve as a visual language of symbols, archetypes, and narratives that help us tap into our intuition and communicate clearly with Source.

When seeking guidance from Mary, Star of the Sea, you might select a tarot card to focus your prayer. For instance, the Star card in tarot could represent Mary in her role as a celestial guide. As you meditate on this card, you can formulate your prayer, asking for guidance in aligning your personal desires with the collective need.

Consider: Where do you want guidance today?

Card Reflection: Channeling Mary, Star of the Sea

Shuffle your tarot deck with the intention of seeking guidance from Mary, Star of the Sea.

Draw one card and place it in front of you. Then, reflect on the card's imagery and how it might relate to your current situation. Formulate a prayer based on your reflections, asking Mary for guidance and clarity.

Mary, Star of the Sea, serves as a spiritual compass, guiding us toward a life that balances personal fulfillment with societal harmony. Through prayer and tools like tarot cards, we can strengthen our connection to the collective.

Affirmation

My guides surround me, always, in the service of Divine Love.

ENCOUNTERING MYSTERY WITH PLUTO IN AQUARIUS

As Pluto embarks on its journey through Aquarius, we are presented with the opportunity to engage in meaningful reflection. This celestial shift invites us to delve into the mysteries that lie within us and around us. It is a call to embark on an expedition into the unknown, driven by curiosity and the desire for discovery.

The encounter with mystery mirrors the process of repentance. It invites us to explore our shadows, acknowledge our missteps, seek forgiveness, and integrate parts of us that we have yet to include. This cosmic alignment prompts us to reassess our actions, aligning them with authenticity and meant to serve the greatest good for all.

However, as Pluto reminds us, genuine transformation is not instantaneous. It is a gradual process, much like composting. As organic matter requires time to decompose and transform into nutrient-rich soil, we too must provide ourselves with the space and time to dismantle old patterns and beliefs. It is in this period of rest and rejuvenation that we can rise anew, ready to sow the seeds of change in our personal landscapes enriched by introspection and self-awareness.

In essence, the transit of Pluto in Aquarius is a journey of personal evolution. It is a path where mystery guides us, reconciliation heals us, and surrender, redirection, and self-correction serve as tools for our healing. It is a time when we are called to not only mend ourselves but also each other and the world at-large. As we navigate this transformative period, let us embrace the opportunity to grow, evolve, and contribute positively to our collective future.

One-Card Spread for Embracing the Mystery with the Three-Second Rule

The Three-Second Rule is a powerful tool that can help you harness your intuition, often referred to as your sixth sense. This rule suggests that within three seconds of having an instinctual thought or feeling, one should act on it.

The concept behind this rule is simple: our intuitive thoughts and feelings, those that appear almost instantly in response to a situation or decision, are often the most authentic and insightful. They are the raw, unfiltered voice of our subconscious mind. However, we frequently dismiss these initial reactions as they can be overshadowed by doubt, overthinking, or fear of judgment.

Here's how you can use the Three-Second Rule to connect with and enhance your sixth sense:

1. **Acknowledge Your First Thought:** The moment a situation arises or a decision needs to be made, pay attention to your initial thought or feeling. This is your intuition speaking.

2. **Hesitate Not:** Instead of questioning, doubting, or dismissing this initial reaction, honor it. You have three seconds to act on it. This could mean voicing

your initial thought, following your gut feeling, or making a decision based on this immediate instinct.

3. **Reflect on the Outcome:** After you've acted on your intuition, take the time to reflect on the outcome. Was your initial instinct accurate or helpful? The more you practice, the more you'll start understanding the contours of your intuition and the language it speaks.

4. **Practice Regularly:** Like any other skill, tapping into your sixth sense requires practice. Make a conscious effort to apply the Three-Second Rule in different aspects of your life, be it personal relationships, professional decisions, or personal growth choices.

Remember, this doesn't mean you should make hasty decisions without considering the consequences, especially in critical or complex situations. It's about learning to trust and recognize your intuitive voice, which is often drowned out by the noise of overthinking or external influences.

Shuffle your card deck while focusing on the question, "What mystery am I being called to explore?" Draw one card and reflect on its meaning. How does this card relate to your current situation? What insights or guidance does it offer you on your journey of transformation?

Affirmation

I embrace the mysteries of life with curiosity and courage. I have learned how to navigate with the sun by day, and the moon and stars by night. I evolve and adapt and move instinctively between control and surrender to that which is beyond my perception.

RELEASING EMOTIONS WITH THE KNIGHT OF CUPS

The Holy Grail myth, intertwined with the legends of the Knights of Avalon and the mythical land of Avalon, has captivated imaginations for centuries. The origin of this enduring myth can be traced back to medieval Arthurian legends and Celtic folklore. At the heart of the myth lies the quest for a sacred chalice, the Holy Grail, which is believed to possess spiritual power and divine grace. The Grail is often associated with Christ's Last Supper and has been imbued with mystical properties, such as the ability to heal or grant eternal life. The Knights of Avalon, including famous figures like King Arthur and Sir Galahad, embark on a noble and perilous quest to find this coveted artifact, representing their spiritual journey and search for enlightenment.

The mythology surrounding the Holy Grail and the Knights of Avalon has been shaped by various historical influences. The story gained popularity during the Middle Ages, reflecting the religious fervor of the time and the fascination with chivalry and honor. Over the years, numerous literary works have contributed to the enduring appeal of the myth. Notably, the 12th-century prose romances, such as Chrétien de Troyes's "Perceval," Wolfram von Eschenbach's "Parzival," and Thomas Malory's "Le Morte d'Arthur," have played a significant role in establishing the core elements of the Holy Grail myth that continue to resonate with audiences today.

The allure of the Holy Grail myth lies in its blend of historical fiction and fantasy. It offers a rich tapestry of adventure, spirituality, and symbolism. The quest for the Grail represents the eternal search for meaning, purpose, and transcendence. It speaks to our deepest desires for spiritual fulfillment and the pursuit of higher ideals. Whether through literature, film adaptations, or modern-day retellings, the Holy Grail myth continues to captivate fans of historical fiction and fantasy, inviting them to embark on a mythical journey that explores the complexities of faith, honor, and the human condition.

Exercise: Finding Your Holy Grail

Begin by reflecting on the emotional build-up you're currently experiencing. Write freely about what emotions are surfacing and why they might be present. Now, imagine these emotions as a hidden treasure or a Holy Grail. What does this "Grail" look like? What does it represent? Write a detailed description. Identify three symbols that represent obstacles or challenges you've encountered on your quest. Describe each symbol and write about what it represents. Reflect on moments of rest and revelation in your journey. How have these moments contributed to your healing process? Finally, write a letter to yourself from the perspective of having found your "Grail." What wisdom and insights would you share with your past self?

Card Reflection: The Grail Healing Journey

Shuffle your deck and lay out six cards side by side.

1. **The Quest:** Represents the current emotional build-up or issue you're facing.

2. **The Grail:** Symbolizes the hidden insight or healing that this issue can lead to.

3. **The Obstacle:** Represents the main challenge or obstacle in your healing journey.

4. **The Knight's Strength:** Indicates the strength or resource you have that will help you overcome this obstacle.

5. **The Moment of Rest:** Suggests how you can find rest and rejuvenation during this journey.

6. **The Revelation:** Reveals the wisdom or insight you'll gain through this healing process.

PISCES III: THE WAY
OF THE ROSE

EARTH PEOPLE

The popular saying that men are from Mars and women are from Venus reflects the perceived differences between the two genders. However, on Earth, we have *people* and we recognize that gender is not limited to a binary perspective. We celebrate the beautiful spectrum of identities fostering inclusivity and acceptance of all gender expressions. Gender is a mere reflection of our internal point of energetic equilibrium. Just like all reactions have different equilibrium points, all people have different points of equilibrium between yang and yin, masculine and feminine, the exchange of conscious energy as the sum of chemical reactions between their left and right brains.

While acknowledging our different equilibrium points, it is essential to remember that no matter our differences, we are all interconnected as beings from Earth. Our shared planet, shared moon, shared stars, and shared sun unite us, transcending borders.

And when we turn our gaze to a common point of reference, the Sun, we give collective gratitude for the mighty celestial body that gifts us with warmth and sustenance. Its radiant energy fuels life on Earth, making it the only known planet where life flourishes. As we bask in the sun's golden rays, let us not take for granted the delicate balance that allows our existence. Instead, let us cherish and protect our Earth home, for—at least in the present moment—there is no "planet B."

In this intricate web of interconnectedness, we find a powerful message: We are called to appreciate the beauty of our unique planet, recognizing the significance of neurodiversity, which includes the expression of gender and energetic preferences, just as the Vesica Piscis symbolizes the harmonious union of masculine and feminine energies both within ourselves and in the collective at-large.

The Vesica Piscis is an ancient symbol, formed by overlapping circles representing the creative power when solar and lunar energies come together to synergize and create. It holds deep significance in spiritual and meditative practices, reminding us of the harmony that arises when the active and receptive energies flow, in a give-and-take, equilibrated dance.

In this vast cosmic expanse, our home stands out as a precious gem, teeming with life and wonder. As stewards of this planet, it is our responsibility to safeguard its delicate ecosystems and nurture its boundless beauty. Together, let us forge a future where gratitude, inclusivity, and preservation guide our actions, ensuring that the legacy we leave for future generations is one of unity and reverence for all living beings.

Exercise: Sacred Geometry in Musical Form, Hallelujah and the Vesica Piscis

Hallelujah is a powerful expression of praise, joy, or thanks used across various spiritual practices. When you listen to Handel's "Hallelujah" chorus, you're not just hearing beautiful music; you're experiencing the audial embodiment of the Vesica Piscis—the integration of energies across the musical spectrum to bring new life into the world in whatever form it seeks to take. Take some time to listen to the chorus. Let the music wash over you and focus on the choral parts that resonate with you the most. After you listen:

- **Reflect:** How did the music make you feel? Did certain parts remind you of the Vesica Piscis and its symbolism?

- **Connect:** Draw connections between your feelings and the meaning of "Hallelujah." Write about how the song's joyous praise relates to unity, creation, and transcendence in your own life.

- **Explore:** Delve deeper into the symbolism of the Vesica Piscis. How does this sacred geometry manifest in your experiences, relationships, or spirituality?

- **Introspect:** Finally, what insights or emotions surfaced during this exercise. How can you apply these insights to your personal growth journey?

Card Reflection: Decan Walk

One of the ways we can embody the spirit of praise and worship of solar energy is by walking with it. A powerful solar journey, known as the Decan Walk—is a profound tool for self-reflection, healing, and deepening our connection with the solar wisdom of astrology and the tarot.

A Decan Walk as a storytelling tool involves drawing cards from a deck to inspire and guide the creation of a narrative. Each card represents a decan—an astrological segment—bringing unique energy, symbolism, and themes into your storytelling journey. It's a wonderful way to infuse your writing with fresh perspectives and unexpected twists.

To begin your Decan Walk, follow these instructions:

- **Select Your Deck:** Choose a deck of cards that resonates with you. While traditional tarot decks work well, you may also explore oracle decks or any combination of decks that speak to your creative spirit.

- **Set Your Intention:** Before diving into the walk, set your intention for the story you wish to create. Whether it's a specific genre, theme, or character-driven narrative, clarifying your intention will focus your energy during the process.

- **Characters:** Each card can represent a character or archetype in your story. Consider the personalities, motivations, and conflicts associated with each decan card. Use them as a foundation for developing rich and multidimensional characters.

- **Plot and Themes:** The energy and symbolism of the decan cards can shape your story's plot and themes. Reflect on the messages conveyed by each card and explore how they intertwine and evolve throughout your narrative.

- **Conflict and Resolution:** Each card may suggest challenges or obstacles that your protagonists face. Use these challenges to create tension and drive your story forward. Likewise, explore how the cards' meanings offer resolutions or lessons for your characters to overcome their struggles.

- Even if you decide against walking with the sun through the decans, the Decan Walk exercise is an excellent tool for breaking writer's block and generating fresh ideas. When you feel stuck or need inspiration, simply perform a Decan Walk with a specific intention related to your current project. Allow the cards to guide and ignite your imagination, infusing new perspectives and unexpected twists into your writing.

Affirmation

The sun inspires my creations.

THE HOLY GRAIL IS IN THE EMERALD CITY

Emerald, a hue that captures the heart with its blend of blue and green, paints a picture of green pastures, fields brimming with life, and a world lush with vegetation. The color emerald is an embodiment of all things vibrant and full of life, much like a landscape drenched in the morning sun, teeming with verdancy.

Colors have a profound effect on our emotions, with each hue possessing the ability to stir different feelings within us. Emerald, with its soothing qualities, is akin to a tranquil green field under a clear sky, offering a sense of peace and balance that is as refreshing as a gentle breeze.

Often associated with matters of the heart, emerald resonates with the feelings of love, compassion, and empathy. Just as a lush green forest invites you to lose yourself in its depths, embracing this color encourages these emotions to surface, allowing us to connect more deeply with ourselves and others.

The color emerald also symbolizes finding one's place or returning home, much like a tree finding its roots deep within the rich, fertile soil. It represents the comfort and harmony of belonging, of being part of the vast green tapestry of life.

Remember the fabled city with streets paved with gold? The Quest for the Holy Grail? Perhaps it's time to reimagine it. Instead of gold, imagine streets paved with lush green, a city where every boulevard is a cascade of emerald, every corner a burst of vibrant life. This is the Emerald City, a symbol from L. Frank Baum's *The Wonderful Wizard of Oz*. In our lives, creating our personal "Emerald City" means crafting an environment that feels safe, loved, and fulfilling. It's about building a sanctuary that reflects your true self.

As we journey through life, the color emerald can serve as more than just a hue. Let it guide us toward love, compassion, and belonging. Let it inspire us to create our own Emerald City, a sanctuary where our hearts truly resonate. Embrace emerald and its healing power, a power that exists because of the radiance of the Sun.

Exercise: Passing into Your Emerald City

Describe your personal Emerald City. What does it look like? Is it a physical place, a state of mind, or perhaps a combination of both? How does being in your Emerald City make you feel? What steps do you need to take to reach your Emerald City? What obstacles might you encounter on your journey to your Emerald City and how can you overcome them? Reflect on a past rite of passage. How did it change you and what did it teach you?

Card Reflection: The Verdant Green Road

Shuffle your deck and lay out six cards side by side.

1. Your current state or where you are now in your journey.

2. The path you're taking toward your Emerald City.

3. The potential challenges that you might face along this path.

4. The tools or strengths you possess.

5. The support you may need to request on your journey.

6. The next steps you need to take.

THE ROSE AND THE SUN AS DIVINE
LOVE WITH THE ACE OF CUPS

As I sit in my garden, savoring the warmth of the sun and admiring the blooming roses, I am reminded of how interconnected everything is. The rose, a symbol of love, needs the sun, its source of energy, to bloom into its full beauty. This relationship between the rose and the sun serves as a beautiful metaphor for Divine Love and how we can attract it into our lives.

The Ace of Cups tarot card, the final cup in this Decan Walk, is a powerful symbol of love, emotional abundance, and spiritual fulfillment. It represents the beginning of a new emotional journey and the awakening of deep feelings of love and compassion. The card often portrays an overflowing cup, signifying the endless source of love from which one can draw.

The association between Mary Magdalene and the Ace of Cups card arises from her strong connection to love and compassion. In some traditions, she is considered the embodiment of Divine Love and the feminine aspect of spirituality. Her story is intertwined with themes of repentance, devotion, and profound love for Jesus, making her a symbol of emotional and spiritual transformation.

The symbolism of the Ace of Cups card reflects Mary Magdalene's character and story. Just as the cup overflows with love, Mary Magdalene's love for Jesus and her unwavering devotion overflowed from her heart. She represents the renewal and rejuvenation of emotions, encouraging individuals to embrace their capacity for love, forgiveness, and spiritual growth. Within Christianity, Mary Magdalene is a prominent figure known as one of the disciples of Jesus Christ. Over time, a rich tapestry of symbolism has emerged associating her with the rose. This connection can be traced back to medieval Christian traditions, where Mary Magdalene was often depicted holding a rose in religious art. The rose came to represent her unconventional purity, beauty, and devotion to Christ.

The rose, with its delicate petals and intoxicating fragrance, has long been a symbol of love. Its beauty evokes feelings of love, passion, and admiration. Yet, without the energy of the sun, the rose would remain a tightly closed bud, never revealing its full potential.

Similarly, Divine Love—the purest, most selfless form of love—is like the Sun. It is a constant, radiant source of warmth and light that enables us to grow and flourish. Just as the rose opens itself to receive the sun's energy, we too must open our hearts to receive Divine Love.

But how do we do this?

Firstly, we must recognize our innate worthiness. Just as the rose doesn't question whether it deserves the sun's light, we must not doubt our worthiness of love. Remember, you are deserving of love simply because you exist. As the famous poet Rumi once said, "Your task is not to seek for love, but merely to seek and find all the barriers within yourself that you have built against it."

Secondly, we need to cultivate self-love. We cannot pour from an empty cup; thus, we must first fill our own cups with love. Practice self-care, set healthy boundaries, and honor your needs and feelings. Self-love isn't selfish; self-love clearly communicates to others where you stand so they can honestly decide where they stand too.

Thirdly, practice openness and vulnerability. Allow yourself to be seen, to be authentic, and to express your true feelings. It may feel scary at first, but vulnerability is the birthplace of deep connection and Divine Love.

And lastly, embody love. Be kind, compassionate, and understanding toward others. Remember, what we give out, we attract back into our lives. Give without expectation of return. Give because it is a moral imperative of the heart.

Attracting Divine Love isn't about sitting back and waiting for it to magically appear. While the invitation to Divine Love is ever-present and irrevocable, like any good contract, it requires acceptance and an exchange of value. That value is our conscious effort and intention. Every day. With every inhale and exhale we align ourselves with the energy of love. And when we're not in that energy—we just adjust and come back to center.

If the idea of Divine Love is new to you, perhaps you could start by setting aside a few minutes each day to meditate on love. Visualize love flowing into you, filling every cell of your body, and then radiating out from you into the world. You could also practice gratitude for the love already present in your life, whether it's the love of family and friends, the love you have for the activities that bring you joy, or even the simple, everyday acts of love like a warm cup of coffee or tea, or a beautiful sunset. But also don't forget love for those who live lives very different from yours—those who are struggling, who don't have basic resources to meet their needs. How can we reinvest our overflow into their communities in a way that honors and respects their humanity while believing in their ability to know how to best take care of themselves?

Divine Love is a contract but isn't just a contract—it is also a covenant.

A relationship that transcends explanation.

Divine Love, like the Sun, is always there, ready to nourish and help us bloom. All we must do is open our hearts, just like the rose opens its petals, ready to receive. Receiving, for some, seems like a very simple thing. But for those who have been repeatedly told they were not worthy of receiving, this recognition and acceptance of Divine Love, is the healing delivered on this journey.

In today's rapidly evolving global community, we encounter a variety of challenges, but we also have a wealth of diverse solutions at our disposal. Jesus's teaching emphasized serving others through Divine Love, aiming for the greatest benefit to all, akin to how the Sun serves us daily. It provides warmth and light, essential elements for our survival. When we face problems, such as the sun's heat being trapped in our atmosphere (due to human-created conditions), perhaps the issue lies in our forgetfulness to appreciate the Sun—its healing energy, its rays, and the rhythm of its rise and fall, in its mirror in the lunar cycles.

In our modern world, where offices and artificial lighting dominate, and our focus is often drawn more toward human-made achievements than expressing gratitude for natural gifts provided to us, we may unintentionally overlook the Sun. Stephen Covey, in *The 7 Habits of Highly Effective People*, offers an analogy of the goose who lays golden eggs. We must not search for the golden eggs while neglecting the goose that produces them. Similarly, we shouldn't yearn for sustenance and care while failing to honor the Sun and its requirements of both comfort and challenge.

And so, as we work together to flow with our ever-evolving global community, let us see challenges as opportunities, knowing that we have an array of diverse solutions within our reach.

May we remember and bring back into the wild of the People, the teachings of Jesus, the Piscean, highlighting the significance of serving others through Divine Love, while using his teachings to have *power with* instead of *power over.*

And may you be filled with the warmth and beauty of Divine Love, living a life as vibrant and beautiful as an emerald garden blooming with roses living under the radiance of the Sun.

And so it is.

WITH GRATITUDE . . .

The cover may have my name, but this book is a collective effort. To this end, I wish to specifically acknowledge and dedicate the following decans to certain individuals and organizations for their unique contributions to the material, teachings, and exercises contained within these pages: "I am, because we are; and since we are, therefore I am."

The Decans of Aries. To Reid Tracy and Kelly Notaras, who generously invest their wisdom, knowledge, and resources into the Hay House Writer's Community. Without your workshop and accountability framework, this book might never have come to fruition, especially as a mother of two young children. Thank you for believing in this book. To the team at KN Literary Arts: Your coaching, support, and structure were integral to the creation of this book. You transformed my list of "random life events" by helping brainstorm an outline for practical application. And finally, to the team at Hay House who assisted me in birthing this book—particularly editor Anna Cooperberg and copyeditor Lea Galanter, who demonstrated grace and patience throughout my editing process.

The Decans of Taurus. My deepest gratitude goes out to all healthcare professionals, both from conventional and alternative medicine, who have lent me their knowledge and strength during my most vulnerable times. Specifically, I want to recognize Dr. Bobbie Stowe from Functional Medicine of Texas, acupuncturists Chris Axelrad and Vy Hoang of the Axelrad Clinic, chiropractors Scott Balin from Katy Wellness Center, and Caroline Long from West University Wellness. I am also grateful for herbalists Katja

Swift, Ryn Midura, and "doctors from a distance" Dr. Mark Hyman and Dr. Deepak Chopra. A special thank-you goes to my dental team, Dr. Tom Hall, Dr. Terry Taylor, and Dr. Tri M. Le, for helping me clear years of trauma manifested in my jaw and teeth. To Dr. Lauren Averbuch—my freshman year roommate who started with me on the path of healing. To Najmeh Mahani—thank you for listening when no one else would. Damon Bethea from Temple Fitness—for teaching me how to connect my mind with my body. And finally, Dr. Corey Clifford and Dr. Mina Sinacori, for their expertise in the art and science of preeclamptic C-section timing.

The Decans of Gemini. My deepest gratitude is extended to Amar, my friend, mentor, and spiritual guide on this journey. I would not be here if it was not for you consistently showing up. The humor and authenticity you infused into your spiritual teachings were the perfect remedy for my healing journey. You remained steadfast and committed, regardless of the number of viewers or followers who reciprocated. To you, I offer a very special, "I am because you are." It's your time, and I pray that all your dreams come true, because the world needs your medicine. Also, to all my pageant sisters and director Shelia Milner who taught me how to discern the right earrings, when you have hundreds to choose from.

The Decans of Cancer. To the women in my lineage who had the courage and fortitude to endure circumstances much harder than my own. To my mother, who taught me from a young age humility, hard and honest work, being authentically myself, and always returning to love and honor, even when you are mistreated. To my grandmother, who helped me explore the more creative parts of myself—and for always having a sewing kit, ice cream, and TV recordings of *I Love Lucy* every Sunday after church. To my sister, Priscilla, and sisters-in-law Jessie and Megan. And to the Cancerian authors who nurtured me from a distance through their words so I could be empowered to share mine: Rebecca Campbell, Gabrielle Bernstein, and Louise Hay. Finally, a thank-you to my daughter, Gabriella—your creativity, curiosity, freedom, friendliness, and joy at exploring the world inspires me to make sure I do what I can do to make your world a little bit easier than the one I endured. You bring a smile and laugh to everyone you meet. I am so honored that you chose me to your "mama."

The Decans of Leo. To my father and all the father-like figures who have been the embodiment of the divine masculine. To my father, who taught me how to see the world in symbols and interpret the signs. We didn't have as much as other families, but he showed me that wealth is not always measured in dollars and cents, but the relationship you have with God the Father, God the Son, and God the Holy Spirit. You lived and breathed the Bible in our household; sometimes I didn't like it, but ultimately, I think it was net positive. You put many boundaries on my life, but it was done in Love, and I trust in Divine Timing and Purpose.

To Pastor Lusk: I was just a young girl in a tiny one-room country church by the river, captivated by your tales of Liberty University in "Lynchhberg Vergina." I was moved by your storytelling prowess, the love and joy you expressed for your congregation, and your appreciation for rock 'n' roll music. While I sometimes got distracted and focused on reassembling my grandma's pens, I'll always remember the sermon where you shared a practical tip for navigating life, advising that during the darkest moments, to "let peace be your umpire." That advice has guided me ever since. Thank you.

To Pastor Joel Osteen, the "pastor with the annoying Southern accent": I used to flip past your sermons while channel surfing and drinking wine while I skipped class in college. Little did I know that years later, I would be assigned to Houston as a Teach for America corps member, living in a hotel directly across from the former Compaq Center, now known as "Lakewood Church." I arrived as a headstrong activist seeking a free marriage license but left as a Proverbs 31 woman forever changed. No one else could have gotten me into church during that season of my life, but you did. You taught me the *power* of "I declare . . ." and your repetition, intonation, and consistent sermon delivery seared the *Sun* onto my heart—in Houston, Texas, the Energy Capital of the World, nonetheless. *"For I know the plans that I have for you . . . plans to prosper you and not to harm you, plans to give you a hope and a future."*

To my brothers, Anthony and Josh, thank you for your unwavering and loving support, even if it is from a distance. Thank you for your dedication to our country and its national security through your service in our armed forces. I may not say it enough, but I am so honored and proud to be your sister. Thank you for accepting and loving me as I am. Lastly, to my son Elijah—your smile shines like the Sun, and I hope to nurture you in a way that fosters new generational cycles for the men in our family.

The Decans of Virgo. To Spencer Michaud, astrologer, musician, and conservationist. Your meticulous research, keen eye for detail, and your gentle yet firm approach to challenging my viewpoints when necessary are deeply appreciated. I admire the respect you showed by always seeking permission before questioning my positions. Your insightful decans webinars and in-depth astrological readings are truly a remarkable and unparalleled body of astrological research. I pray that you receive all that you desire in exchange for your generous spirit and service to this book and to the world.

The Decans of Libra. To Adam Elenbaas of Nightlight Astrology. Your expertise, storytelling, and unwavering dedication to practicing astrology based on deep knowledge of primary source texts, while maintaining an open and non-judgmental perspective, is unmatched. You're my Cancer-Capricorn reflection—thank you for your enlightening courses, moon circle alongside your wife and herbalist, Ashley, and your insightful podcast that embodies the principles of 1 Corinthians 13. Your guidance has been a beacon of light in my life during this period like no other.

The Decans of Scorpio. To Alex Amorosi, astrologer, Reiki Master teacher, energy worker, yoga teacher, and spiritual coach. Your insights on Black Moon Lilith and Salem, Massachusetts, were instrumental in finalizing the final connections in this book. I am grateful for your unwavering support as I transition from a period of healing to actualizing my ideas into physical reality and grounding myself back to the Earth after some time away.

The Decans of Sagittarius. To all the professors, educators, and institutions that have enriched me as a student and fostered my growth. Specifically, to my piano instructor, Rodney Barnett. One of my cherished memories from our sessions was getting a glimpse into your hobbies—nurturing African violets and restoring old organs. Your invaluable lessons on rubato have served me well throughout my life, reminding me that "The notes on the page are just guides." Thank you also to Teach For America, AmeriCorps, Red Lion Area School District, Houston Independent School District, YES Prep Public Schools, Katy Independent School District, Temple University, Brigham Young University, the State University of New York in Buffalo, University of St. Thomas Houston, South Texas College of Law, University of Houston, and Penn State University. To tarot educators Richard Knight and Bridgit Esselmont. Your efforts have been instrumental in bringing tarot from the hidden corners of incense-filled rooms into the light, dispelling its dark age mystique. My children's Montessori teachers—I couldn't have written this book without you loving my children as much as I do. You are truly exceptional. Thank you. And finally, Dr. Kyriakos Kontopoulous, who called me out in front of the entire class, telling me the reason I wasn't at Harvard University was because I didn't ask questions. I've been asking questions ever since.

The Decans of Capricorn. To my law professors, business mentors, associates, and all who have been friends and allies in this work. Specifically, to Ali Katz of Personal Family Lawyer and Tracey Hester. Also, to my 1L professors—my success on the bar exam was because of your "old school" ways—Charles "Rocky" Rhodes, Vanessa Browne-Barbour, Maxine Goodman, Randall Kelso, Fran Ortiz, Val Ricks, Dru Stevenson, and Cherie Taylor. And finally, to "Teach for America Domain 3 plus honorary members," Kellie Thompson, Krissy Watson, Selina Hall, Joshua Gutierrez, Kevin Puckett, Sarah Straub, Louise Matherne (Burgher), Jose Montijo, Courtney Bell, Stephanie Gounder, Johnie Flores, Stephen Perrault, Johnny Solis, Logan Quinn, and Zac Dearing. If I ever become president of the United States, y'all will be my

Department of Education. So many lessons contained in this book came from our relationships, prayers, and experiences. I believe we were brought together during that time for a unique purpose, and even though time and distance separate us, I'm sure KP will always be down to organize a "party with a purpose," under a private calendar invite, bcc, of course. Also, thank you to my business mentors Sam Ovens and Richard Knight.

And finally, to Peter. We had a chance encounter at McDonald's my senior year of high school and a chance encounter at a Starbucks the last night I was working on this book. Just like our first meeting, that second meeting was also meant to be. Given that this is a book arranged and inspired by the Egyptian solar calendar, I would like to think you had something to do with that. You introduced me to Christian mysticism and I witnessed miracles, even though, at the time, I was too young to believe. You taught me the power of believing in myself, dreaming big, having a mind for business, and being of service to others. You always accepted me, just as I was, until it was time for us to part ways. We share a story of religious persecution, in different ways, and I pray that one day you will be able to return home to Egypt and reconcile yours.

The Decans of Aquarius. To Alex. Our relationship has covered the entirety of the Zodiac, and yet, here we are. During the first week we met, we stayed up all night, so many nights, and just talked about our lives—it was like I had found family without knowing you were family. You inspire me with your focus and single-minded dedication to mastering your craft—whether it be lawyering, chess, being a father, woodworking, football drafts, or fantasy sports. You are, by far, the *most* calculating and strategic person I have ever met. And your negotiation skills are unparalleled. You challenge my thinking in a way I don't always like but have grown to appreciate. This book would not have been possible without you—your love, your exceptional financial provision, your openness to considering my ideas, your proactiveness with our children. I was able to heal deep childhood wounds in large part because of your consistency and dedication to showing up, no matter what. You carry a great capacity to Love and I pray that you become all you desire to become.

The Decans of Pisces. And finally, to the One who lights my soul on fire. He doesn't look a thing like Jesus, but sometimes, with the right lighting, he does. My Heart has been tuned to the Music of your Soul. Thank you for being the Love I always imagined when I was young. Time and chance may happen to us all, but sometimes it feels like time has stopped and Eternity is right next door. There are many kinds of Love, and never the same Love twice. I am so grateful that Ours gets to be This. You're the Sun to my Moon, my First and my Last—Always and Forever Yours . . . Thank you for being the Key that Liberated my Soul.

"When everything's made to be broken, I just want you to know who I am . . ."

RESOURCES BY DECAN

Aries

Astro-Charts.com. "Homepage." Accessed October 10, 2023. https://astro-charts.com/.

AstroGold. "Get AstroGold." Accessed October 10, 2023. https://www.astrogold.io/.

Corcos, Christine. "Seeing It Coming since 1945: State Bans and Regulations of Crafty Sciences Speech and Activity." *LSU Law Digital Commons*, Journal Articles 37, no. 1 (Fall 2014): 39–114. https://digitalcommons.law.lsu.edu/faculty_scholarship/400.

Coué, Émile. *Self Mastery Through Conscious Autosuggestion*. London: George Allen & Unwin Ltd, 1920.

Frankel, Tamar and Tomasz Braun. "Law and Culture." *Boston University Law Review Online* 157 (2021), https://www.bu.edu/bulawreview/2021/12/30/law-and-culture/.

Haines, Staci K. *The Politics of Trauma: Somatics, Healing, and Social Justice*. Berkeley, CA: North Atlantic Books, 2019.

Hay, Louise. *Power Thought Cards: A 64-Card Deck*. Carlsbad, CA: Hay House, Inc., 1999.

Jung, C. G. *The Undiscovered Self: With Symbols and the Interpretation of Dreams*. Princeton, NJ: Princeton University Press, 1990.

Kaplan, Diane S. *An Introduction to the American Legal System, Government, and Constitutional Law*. Frederick, MD: Aspen Publishing, 2015.

Manne, Kate. *Down Girl: The Logic of Misogyny*. New York: Oxford University Press, 2018.

McLaren, Brian. *Why Don't They Get It? Overcoming Bias in Others (and Yourself)*. 2019. E-book.

Nagoski, Emily and Amelia Nagoski. *Burnout: The Secret to Unlocking the Stress Cycle*. New York: Ballantine Books, 2019.

Osteen, Joel. *The Power of I Am: Two Words That Will Change Your Life Today*. New York: Faith Words, 2015.

Proof Leadership. "Homepage." Proof Leadership Group. Accessed August 22, 2023. https://proofleadership.com/.

Project Implicit. "Implicit Association Test." Project Implicit. Accessed October 10, 2023. https://implicit.harvard.edu/implicit/takeatest.html.

van der Kolk, Bessel. *The Body Keeps the Score: Brain, Mind, and Body in the Healing of Trauma*. New York: Viking, 2014.

Taurus

Ayales, Adriana and Josephine Klerks. *The Herbal Astrology Oracle: A 55-Card Deck and Guidebook*. Carlsbad, CA: Hay House, Inc., 2022.

Booth, Martin. *Cannabis: A History*. New York: Picador, 2005.

Cameron, Julia. *The Artist's Way*. New York: TarcherPerigee, 1992.

Clark Strand and Perdita Finn. *The Way of the Rose: The Radical Path of the Divine Feminine Hidden in the Rosary*. New York: Random House, 2019.

Kimmerer, Robin Wall. *Braiding Sweetgrass: Indigenous Wisdom, Scientific Knowledge and the Teachings of Plants*. Minneapolis, MN: Milkweed Editions, 2013.

LePera, Dr. Nicole. *How to Do the Work: Recognize Your Patterns, Heal from Your Past, and Create Your Self*. New York: Harper Wave, 2020.

Marians of the Immaculate Conception. "How to Recite the Rosary." July 29, 2021. https://marian.org/mary/rosary/how-to-pray.

Marie, Tania. *Spiritual Skin: Sacred Tattoos: More than Skin Deep*. Createspace Independent Publishing Platform, 2011.

Seshadri, Krishna G. "The Neuroendocrinology of Love." *Indian Journal of Endocrinology and Metabolism* 20, no. 4 (July–August 2016): 558–63. https://doi.org/10.4103/2230-8210.183479.

Gemini

Amen Clinics. "Why Are We so Negative?" *Amen Clinics Blog*. Accessed August 23, 2023. https://www.amenclinics.com/blog/why-are-we-so-negative/.

East Bay Meditation Center. "Agreements for Multicultural Interactions at EBMC." *East Bay Meditation Center Blog*. Accessed August 23, 2023. https://eastbaymeditation.org/2022/03/agreements-for-multicultural-interactions/.

Craske, Michelle G. and David H. Barlow. *Mastery of Your Anxiety and Worry: Workbook*. 2nd ed. New York: Oxford University Press, 2006.

Hay, Louise. *You Can Heal Your Life*. Carlsbad, CA: Hay House, Inc., 2022.

Holland, John. *The Psychic Tarot Oracle Cards*. Carlsbad, CA: Hay House, Inc., 2009.

Moore, Thomas. *Dark Nights of the Soul: A Guide to Finding Your Way Through Life's Ordeals*. New York: Gotham Books, 2004.

Nowicki, Stephen. *Choice or Chance: Understanding Your Locus of Control and Why It Matters*. Buffalo, NY: Prometheus Books, 2016.

Stone, Douglas, Bruce Patton, and Sheila Heen. *Difficult Conversations: How to Discuss What Matters Most*. New York: Penguin Books, 2010.

Toyoshima, K., H. Fukui, and K. Kuda. "Piano Playing Reduces Stress More Than Other Creative Art Activities." *International Journal of Music Education* 29, no. 3 (2011): 257–263. https://doi.org/10.1177/0255761411408505.

Cancer

Arney, Jane. "The Song of Miriam." *Seeing God in Art*. January 21, 2015. https://seeinggodinart.wordpress.com/2015/01/21/the-song-of-miriam/.

Campbell, Brian. *Many Lives, Many Masters*. New York: Touchstone, 2012.

Campbell, Rebecca. *Healing Waters Oracle*. Carlsbad, CA: Hay House, Inc., 2023.

Campbell, Rebecca. *Rise Sister Rise*. Carlsbad, CA: Hay House, Inc., 2016.

Eleni, Sophia. *Breaking the Cycle*. London: Perspective Press Global, 2022.

Greene, Liz and Howard Sasportas. *The Luminaries*. Boston: Weiser, 1992.

Kaehr, Shelley A. *Heal Your Ancestors to Heal Your Life*. Woodbury, MN: Llewellyn Publications, 2021.

Louie, Dexter, Karolina Brook, and Elizabeth Frates. "The Laughter Prescription: A Tool for Lifestyle Medicine." *American Journal of Lifestyle Medicine* 10, no. 4 (July/August 2016). https://www.ncbi.nlm.nih.gov/pmc/articles/PMC6125057/.

Nepo, Mark. *Seven Thousand Ways to Listen: Staying Close to What is Sacred*. New York: Atria Books, 2012.

Leo

Blanch, Andrea and Kimberly Konkel. "Creating Trauma-Informed Congregations." *Office on Women's Health Blog*. April 3, 2014. https://www.womenshealth.gov/blog/trauma-informed-congregations.

Campbell, Joseph. *The Hero with a Thousand Faces*. Joseph Campbell Foundation, 2020. E-book.

Covey, Stephen R. *The 7 Habits of Highly Effective People: Powerful Lessons in Personal Change*. New York: Simon & Schuster, 2013.

de Vries, Bert J. M. *Sustainability Science*. Cambridge, UK: Cambridge University Press, 2012.

Fox, Matthew. *The Hidden Spirituality of Men: Ten Metaphors to Awaken the Sacred Masculine*. Novato, CA: New World Library, 2008.

Garcia, Samantha. *Regenerative Business*. Dirty Alchemy Inc, 2023.

Loorz, Victoria. *Church of the Wild*, Minneapolis, MN: Broadleaf Books, 2021.

Osteen, Joel. *The Power of I Am: Two Words That Will Change Your Life Today*. New York: Faith Words, 2015.

Rice, Andrea. "Trauma-Informed Mindfulness: A Guide," PsychCentral. Last modified January 5, 2022. https://psychcentral.com/health/trauma-informed-mindfulness.

Smith, Caroline and John Astrop. *Oracle of the Radiant Sun: Astrology Cards to Illuminate Your Life*. Atglen, PA: Red Feather, 2019.

Smith, Jason E. *Religious but Not Religious: Living a Symbolic Life*. Asheville, NC: Chiron Publications, 2021.

Snyder, Morgan. *Becoming a King: The Path to Restoring the Heart of a Man*. Nashville, TN: W Publishing Group, 2020.

Lavender Healing Collective. "Our Vision." *Lavender Healing Collective*. Accessed October 10, 2023. https://www.lavenderhealingcollective.com.

TherapyNotes and Michelle Moseley. "Healing Religious Trauma and Spiritual Wounds in Private Practice." August 23, 2022. YouTube video. https://www.youtube.com/watch?v=mMQWy7A7MtU.

Tick, Edward. "PTSD: The Sacred Wound." *Journal of the Catholic Health Association of the United States* (May/June 2013). https://www.chausa.org/publications/health-progress/article/may-june-2013/ptsd-the-sacred-wound.

Virgo

Baron, Josh and Lachenauer, Rob. *Harvard Business Review Family Business Handbook: How to Build and Sustain a Successful, Enduring Enterprise*. Boston: Harvard Business Review Press, 2021.

Covey, Stephen R. *The 7 Habits of Highly Effective Families: Creating a Nurturing Family in a Turbulent World*. New York: Golden Press, 2022.

D'Argent, Victor. *An Uncommon Way to Wealth*. Dublin: Charterhouse Publishing, 1994.

Hill, Napoleon. *The Law of Success*. New York: TarcherPerigee, 2017.

Hughes, James E. *Complete Family Wealth: Wealth as Well-Being*. New York: Bloomberg Press, 2021.

Personal Family Lawyer, www.personalfamilylawyer.com.

Tarnas, Richard. *Cosmos and Psyche: Intimations of a New World View*. New York: Plume, 2006.

Libra

Burton, Tara Isabella. *Strange Rites: New Religions for a Godless World*. New York: Public-Affairs, 2022.

Campion, Nicholas. *Astrology and Popular Religion in the Modern West: Prophecy, Cosmology, and the New Age Movement*. New York: Routledge, 2016.

Fisher, Roger, William Ury, and Bruce Patton. *Getting to Yes: Negotiating Agreement Without Giving In*. New York: Penguin Books, 2011.

George, Demetra and Douglas Block. *Asteroid Goddesses: The Mythology, Psychology, and Astrology of the Re-Emerging Feminine*. Lake Worth, FL: Ibis Press, 2003.

Isaacson, Walter. *Steve Jobs*. New York: Simon & Schuster, 2011.

National Archives. *The Declaration of Independence: A Transcription*. Accessed October 10, 2023. https://www.archives.gov/founding-docs/declaration-transcript.

Smith, Jason E. *Religious but Not Religious: Living a Symbolic Life*. Asheville, NC: Chiron Publications, 2020.

Scorpio

Bernstein, Gabrielle. *Judgment Detox: Release the Beliefs That Hold You Back from Living a Better Life*. New York: Gallery Books, 2018.

Boland, Yasmin. *Moonology Manifestation Oracle*. Carlsbad, CA: Hay House, Inc., 2021.

Boland, Yasmin. *Moonology: Working with the Magic of Lunar Cycles*. Carlsbad, CA: Hay House, Inc., 2016.

Brown, Brené. *Atlas of the Heart: Mapping Meaningful Connection and the Language of Human Experience*. New York: Random House, 2021.

Estés, Clarissa Pinkola. *Women Who Run with the Wolves: Myths and Stories of the Wild Woman Archetype*. New York: Ballantine Books, 1992.

George, Demetra. *Mysteries of the Dark Moon: The Healing Power of the Dark Goddess*, New York: HarperCollins, 1992.

Koch, Liz. *The Psoas Book*. 30th anniversary rev. ed. Felton, CA: Guinea Pig Publications, 2012.

Jenik, Adriene. *The Grief Deck: Rituals, Meditations, and Tools for Moving Through Loss*. Princeton, NJ: Princeton Architectural Press, 2022.

Montalbano, William D. "Vatican Finds Galileo 'Not Guilty.'" *The Washington Post*. November 1, 1992. https://www.washingtonpost.com/archive/politics/1992/11/01/vatican-finds-galileo-not-guilty/1092b119-440e-4fb6-b990-cc7f8a662f0d/.

O'Sullivan, Suzanne. *The Sleeping Beauties: And Other Stories of Mystery Illness*. New York: Pantheon, 2021.

Sédir, Paul. *Occult Botany: Sédir's Concise Guide to Magical Plants*. Rochester, VT: Inner Traditions, 2021.

Smith, Tiffany Watt. *The Book of Human Emotions*. London: Wellcome Collection, 2016.

Tolle, Eckhart. *A New Earth: Awakening to Your Life's Purpose*. New York: Penguin Life, 2006.

Sagittarius

Sacks, Rabbi Jonathan. *Covenant & Conversation: A Weekly Reading of the Jewish Bible, Genesis, the Book of Beginnings*. New Milford, CT: Maggid Books, 2009.

Capricorn

Campbell, Rebecca. *Work Your Light Oracle Cards*. Carlsbad, CA: Hay House, Inc., 2018.

Greene, Liz. *Saturn: A New Look at an Old Devil*. Boston: Weiser Books, 2021.

Hill, Napoleon. *Think and Grow Rich*. New York: TarcherPerigee, 2005.

Michelli, Joseph A. *The New Gold Standard: 5 Leadership Principles for Creating a Legendary Customer Experience Courtesy of The Ritz-Carlton Hotel Company*. New York: McGraw Hill, 2008.

Proctor, Bob. *You Were Born Rich*. 2011. E-book.

Ruback, Richard S. and Royce Yudkoff. *HBR Guide to Buying a Small Business*. Boston: Harvard Business Review Press, 2017.

Wattles, Wallace D. et al. *The Prosperity Bible*. New York: TarcherPerigee, 2012.

Yogananda, Paramhansa. *Autobiography of a Yogi*. Los Angeles: Self-Realization Fellowship, 1998.

Aquarius

Barlow, Dr. Wilfred. *The Alexander Technique: How to Use Your Body Without Stress*. New York: Healing Arts Press, 1991.

Campbell, Rebecca and Danielle Noel. *The Starseed Oracle*. London: Hay House UK, 2020.

DiNicolantonio, Dr. James. *The Salt Fix: Why the Experts Got It All Wrong—and How Eating More Might Save Your Life*. New York: Harmony, 2017.

Elenbaas, Adam. *Fisher of Men: The Gospel of an Ayahuasca Vision Quest*. New York: TarcherPerigee, 2010.

Elkington, David et al. *The Ancient Language of Sacred Sound: The Acoustic Science of the Divine*. Rochester, VT: Inner Traditions, 2021.

Grandin, Temple. *Visual Thinking: The Hidden Gifts of People Who Think in Pictures, Patterns, and Abstractions*. New York: Riverhead Books, 2022.

Hallowell, Edward M. and John J. Ratey. *ADHD 2.0: New Science and Essential Strategies for Thriving with Distraction—from Childhood through Adulthood*. New York: Ballantine Books, 2021.

Hamilton, Heather and Jim Palmer. *Returning to Eden: A Field Guide for the Spiritual Journey*. Chico, CA: Quoir, 2023.

Hyman, Dr. Mark. *Young Forever: The Secrets to Living Your Longest, Healthiest Life*. New York: Little, Brown Spark, 2023.

LePera, Dr. Nicole. *How to Do the Work: Recognize Your Patterns, Heal from Your Past, and Create Your Self*. New York: Harper Wave, 2020.

Talbot, Michael. *The Holographic University: The Revolutionary Theory of Reality*. New York: Harper Perennial, 2011.

Tompkins, Peter and Christopher Bird. *The Secret Life of Plants: A Fascinating Account of the Physical, Emotional, and Spiritual Relations Between Plants and Man*. New York: Harper Paperbacks, 2018.

van der Kolk, Bessel. *The Body Keeps the Score: Brain, Mind, and Body in the Healing of Trauma*. New York: Penguin Books, 2014.

Pisces

Campbell, Rebecca. *The Rose Oracle*. Carlsbad, CA: Hay House, Inc., 2022.

Duguay, Mario. *Healing Energy Oracle*. Woodbury, MN: Llewellyn Publications, 2020.

Fairchild, Alana and Rassouli. *Rumi Oracle: An Invitation into the Heart of the Divine*. Woodbury, MN: Llewellyn Publications, 2016.

Greene, Liz. *The Astrological Neptune and the Quest for Redemption*. Boston: Weiser, 2000.

Marren, Reese. *The Divine Decan Tarot*. Los Angeles: Reese Marren, 2021.

The Church of England. "The Lord's Prayer." Accessed October 10, 2023. https://www.churchofengland.org/our-faith/what-we-believe/lords-prayer.

Watterson, Meggan. *The Mary Magdalene Oracle: A 44-Card Deck & Guidebook of Mary's Gospel & Legend*. Carlsbad, CA: Hay House, Inc., 2023.

TAROT-ASTROLOGY CORRESPONDENCES

Rulership is based on the traditional Chaldean order of the planets: *Saturn, Jupiter, Mars, Sun, Venus, Mercury, Moon.* This is based on a geocentric cosmological model. For more information, consult William Lilly's *Christian Astrology, Book 1: An Introduction to Astrology* and *Book 2: The Resolution of All Manner of Questions.*

	ZODIAC	DECAN	Tarot	RULER	KEYWORD
I AM	**Aries** *Emperor,* *Tower*	Aries I	2 of Wands	Mars	Invite
		Aries II	3 of Wands	Sun	Choose
		Aries III	4 of Wands	Venus	Symbolize
		Queen of Wands			
		Ascendant			
I HAVE	**Taurus** *Empress,* *Emperor*	Taurus I	5 of Pentacles	Mercury	Respond
		Taurus II	6 of Pentacles	Moon	Dissent
		Taurus III	7 of Pentacles	Saturn	Question
		King of Pentacles			
		Page of Pentacles			
I THINK	**Gemini** *The Lovers*	Gemini I	8 of Swords	Jupiter	Redirect
		Gemini II	9 of Swords	Mars	Transform
		Gemini III	10 of Swords	Sun	Surrender
		Knight of Swords			
		Ace of Swords			
	SOLSTICE				
I FEEL	**Cancer** *Chariot,* *High Priestess*	Cancer I	2 of Cups	Venus	Integrate
		Cancer II	3 of Cups	Mercury	Laugh
		Cancer III	4 of Cups	Moon	Birth
		Queen of Cups			
		Descendant			
I WILL	**Leo** *Strength,* *Sun*	Leo I	5 of Wands	Saturn	Collaborate
		Leo II	6 of Wands	Jupiter	Serve
		Leo III	7 of Wands	Mars	Rewild
		King of Wands			
		Page of Wands			
I ANALYZE	**Virgo** *The Hermit*	Virgo I	8 of Pentacles	Sun	Work
		Virgo II	9 of Pentacles	Venus	Rest
		Virgo III	10 of Pentacles	Mercury	Regenerate
		Knight of Pentacles			
		Ace of Pentacles			
	EQUINOX				

	ZODIAC	DECAN	Tarot	RULER	KEYWORD
I BALANCE	Libra *Justice,* *Empress*	Libra I	2 of Swords	Moon	Deconstruct
		Libra II	3 of Swords	Saturn	Agree
		Libra III	4 of Swords	Jupiter	Rise
		Queen of Swords			
I TRANSFORM	Scorpio *Death,* *Judgment*	Scorpio I	5 of Cups	Mars	Lose
		Scorpio II	6 of Cups	Sun	See
		Scorpio III	7 of Cups	Venus	Embrace
		King of Cups			
I SEE	Sagittarius *Temperance,* *Wheel of Fortune*	Sagittarius I	8 of Wands	Mercury	Heal
		Sagittarius II	9 of Wands	Moon	Forgive
		Sagittarius III	10 of Wands	Saturn	Release
		Knight of Wands			
		Ace of Wands			
		SOLSTICE			
I USE	Capricorn *Devil,* *World*	Capricorn I	2 of Pentacles	Jupiter	Establish
		Capricorn II	3 of Pentacles	Mars	Create
		Capricorn III	4 of Pentacles	Sun	Manage
		Queen of Pentacles			
I KNOW	Aquarius *Star, Fool*	Aquarius I	5 of Swords	Venus	Innovate
		Aquarius II	6 of Swords	Mercury	Transpose
		Aquarius III	7 of Swords	Moon	Reorient
		King of Swords			
I DREAM	Pisces *Moon, High* *Priestess*	Pisces I	8 of Cups	Saturn	Return
		Pisces II	9 of Cups	Jupiter	Reconcile
		Pisces III	10 of Cups	Mars	Realize
		Knight of Cups			
		Ace of Cups			
		The Magician			
		EQUINOX			

ABOUT THE AUTHOR

Jackie Hope is a civil rights attorney, tarot reader, musician, and astrologer. She is a 2010 Teach for America alumna who has worked in education reform, environmental justice, and mental health services. As someone who has come through the dark night of activist burnout, Jackie guides changemakers in working through their dark nights using tarot and astrology, so that they can continue to impact their communities for the better.

Hay House Titles of Related Interest

YOU CAN HEAL YOUR LIFE, the movie,
starring Louise Hay & Friends
(available as an online streaming video)
www.hayhouse.com/louise-movie

THE SHIFT, the movie,
starring Dr. Wayne W. Dyer
(available as an online streaming video)
www.hayhouse.com/the-shift-movie

***

WHAT'S YOUR SOUL SIGN?: Astrology for Waking Up,
Transforming and Living a High-Vibe Life by Debbie Frank

Tarot MADE EASY: Learn How to Read and
Interpret the Cards by Kim Arnold

THE WANDERING STAR Tarot: An 80-Card Deck
and Guidebook by Cat Pierce

STARCODES ASTRO ORACLE: A 56-Card Deck
and Guidebook by Heather Roan Robbins

All of the above are available at www.hayhouse.co.uk.

CONNECT WITH
HAY HOUSE
ONLINE

🌐 hayhouse.co.uk   𝐟 @hayhouse

📷 @hayhouseuk   𝕏 @hayhouseuk

▶ @hayhouseuk   ♪ @hayhouseuk

Find out all about our latest books & card decks • Be the first
to know about exclusive discounts • Interact with our authors
in live broadcasts • Celebrate the cycle of the seasons with us
• Watch free videos from your favourite authors •
Connect with like-minded souls

'The gateways to wisdom and knowledge
are always open.'

Louise Hay